Praise for Brian Leaf's *Top 50 Skills* Series

Top 50 Skills for a Top Score: SAT Math

"What a surprise, what a relief! An SAT guide that actually meets you where you are, talks to you with wit and compassion, and clears away the panic of test-taking. And, the writing is first-rate too. Bravo Brian Leaf."

Rebecca Pepper Sinkler, former Editor, *The New York Times Book Review*

"I enjoyed the informal writing style, and the flash cards for math are brilliant! Students are used to stacks of vocabulary words in preparation for the verbal portion of the test, why not drills on flash cards for the math section?"

Denise Brown-Allen, Ed.D., Upper School Director, The Pingry School

"If everyone starts using Brian's secrets and strategies, The College Board and ETS are going to have to rewrite the SAT!!"

Max Shelton, George Washington University, Class of 2012

Top 50 Skills for a Top Score: SAT Critical Reading and Writing

"Brian Leaf has hacked off the head of America's high school boogie man—the dreaded SAT. He clearly lays out how the test works, accessible preparation strategies, and how to maximize one's score. Any college applicant can benefit from his thoughtful and well-researched advice."

Joie Jager-Hyman, former Assistant Director of Admissions, Dartmouth College, author of *Fat Envelope Frenzy: One Year, Five Promising Students and the Pursuit of the Ivy League Prize*

"A long time ago, in an era far, far away, I took the SAT—and I can remember the pressure and anxiety of it like it was yesterday. Lucky for you modern-day seniors, Brian Leaf has written the SAT guide to end all SAT guides. He thoroughly demystifies the test and lays out the 50 skills you need to max out your score. Better yet, Mr. Leaf writes with such humor, wit, and unpretentious expertise that you'll find yourself reading this book just for fun. I did. It almost—almost—even made me want to take the SAT again."

Sora Song, Senior Editor, *Time Magazine*

"What's more scary than facing SATs? Or more boring than prepping for them? For a student swinging wildly between angst and ennui, the solution is Brian Leaf's *Top 50 Skills for a Top Score: SAT Critical Reading and Writing*. Leaf, himself a genius at connecting with teenagers, meets students at their level, and spikes every drill with common sense and comedy. I especially loved the Superbad Vocabulary section—not your usual stuffy approach to language deficit disorder. Guaranteed to relax and engage the most reluctant (or panicked) student."

Rebecca Pepper Sinkler, former Editor, *The New York Times Book Review*

Top 50 Skills for a Top Score: ACT Math

"Anyone even thinking of taking the ACT needs this short but targeted guide to the math section. You simply can't afford not to spend the time reading his laser sharp drills that break down every type of problem on the ACT, show the math behind each type, and then provide drill sections based on that skill set. Even poor math students can learn to recognize all the types of math on the ACT and learn the ropes enough to get most of the easy and medium questions right every time. Mr. Leaf's guide is even entertaining as he gives the skill sets names like "Green Circle, Black Diamond" to make it feel like you are skiing rather than slogging through lessons. If you want a short but concise guide to the ACT with every trick and mathematical explanation necessary to get a perfect score, this is the book for you. You may even actually LEARN real math in the process as Mr. Leaf's love of the subject shines through so you don't just feel you are learning for a test."

Dr. Michele Hernandez, author of the bestselling books *A is for Admission*, *The Middle School Years*, and *Acing the College Application*

"Brian Leaf knows how to talk with students and in his book, *Top 50 Skills for a Top Score: ACT Math*, you can hear his voice loud and clear. Students who follow Brian's "Mantras" and work through the practice questions will gain confidence in their work, as well as improve their ACT scores."

Barbara Anastos, former Director, Monmouth Academy

"Feels like you have an insider divulging secrets from behind the walls of the ACT! At times going so far as to circumvent the math skills themselves, Brian gives practical tips and tricks specifically designed to outwit the ACT's formula, and he does it all with a sense of humor and fun. Nice job!"

Danica McKellar, actress (*The Wonder Years*, *West Wing*) and mathematician and author of *New York Times* bestsellers *Math Doesn't Suck* and *Kiss My Math*

Top 50 Skills for a Top Score: ACT English, Reading, and Science

"This book is a good read even if you *don't* have to take the ACT."

Edward Fiske, author of the bestselling college guide, the *Fiske Guide to Colleges*

"The **specific** skills needed for the ACT, confidence building, stress-management, how to avoid careless errors . . . this book has it covered!"

Laura Frey, Director of College Counseling, Vermont Academy
Former President, New England Association for College Admission Counseling

McGraw-Hill's Top 50 Skills for a Top Score: SAT Math

Brian Leaf, M.A.

New York | Chicago | San Francisco | Lisbon | London | Madrid |
Mexico City | Milan | New Delhi | San Juan Seoul |
Singapore | Sydney | Toronto

The McGraw·Hill Companies

Library of Congress Cataloging-in-Publication Data

Leaf, Brian.
   McGraw-Hill's top 50 skills for a top score: SAT math / by Brian Leaf.
      p. cm.
   "Featuring: over 450 SAT questions; top 50 skills flashcards; special
section: how to break 700."
   Includes bibliographical references and index.
   ISBN-13: 978-0-07-161391-0 (alk. paper)
   ISBN-10: 0-07-161391-9 (alk. paper)
   1.   Mathematics—Examinations—Study   guides.   2.   SAT   (Educational
test)—Study guides.   3.   Universities and colleges—Examinations—Study
guides.   I. Title. II. Title: Top 50 skills for a top score : SAT math.
III. Title: SAT math.
   QA43.L4187 2010
   510.76—dc22

                                                                2008051614

5 6 7 8 9   QDB/QDB   0 1 4 3 2

ISBN: 978-0-07-161391-0
MHID: 0-07-161391-9

Printed and Bound by Quad/Graphics/Dubuque

McGraw-Hill books are available at special quantity discounts to use as
premiums and sales promotions, or for use in corporate training programs.
To contact a representative please e-mail us at bulksales@mcgraw-hill.com.

Contents

How to Use This Book

It's simple. The questions that will appear on your SAT are predictable. Every SAT has a few function questions, one or two ratio questions, an average question, etc. While each of these topics is broad and could be the subject of a whole mathematics course, **the SAT always tests the same concepts!**

In this book, I will teach you exactly what you need to know. I will introduce each topic and follow it with drills. After each set of drills, check your answers. Read and reread the solutions until they make sense. They are designed to simulate one-on-one tutoring, like I'm sitting right there with you. Reread the solutions until you could teach them to a friend. In fact, do that! My students call it "learning to channel their inner Brian Leaf." There is no better way to learn and master a concept than to teach it!

Any new concept that you master will be worth 10 or more points toward you SAT Math score. That's the plan; it is that simple. If you did not understand functions, ratios, and averages before and now you do, you will earn 30+ extra points.

This book is filled with SAT Math Mantras. They tell you what to do and when to do it. "When you see a proportion, cross-multiply." "When you see a linear pair, determine the measures of the angles." This is the stuff that girl who got an 800 on her SAT Math does automatically. The Mantras teach you to think like her.

"Sounds good, but the SAT is tricky," you say. It is, but we know their tricks. Imagine a football team that has great plays, but only a few of them. We could watch films and study those plays. No matter how tricky they are, we could learn them, expect them, and beat them. SAT prep works the same way. You will learn the strategies, expect the SAT's tricks, and raise your score. Now, go learn and rack up the points!

Easy, Medium, Hard, and Guessing

The SAT is not graded like a math test at school. If you got only half the questions right on an algebra midterm, that'd be a big fat F. On the math SAT, half the questions right is a 500, the average score for kids across the country. If you got 70% of the questions right, that'd be a C− in school, but almost a 600 on the SAT, the average score for admission to schools like Goucher and University of Vermont. If you got 89% correct, which is a measly B+ in school, it is a beautiful 700 on the SAT, and about the average for kids who got into Georgetown, U.C. Berkeley, Emory, and Wesleyan.

Use this info to determine how many questions you need to answer on the SAT. The math questions are organized in order of difficulty, from easiest to hardest. If you want half correct, or 70% correct, don't rush through the easies just to get to the hard ones. In school you might need to finish tests in order to do well, here you do not. You only need to get to the very hardest questions if you are shooting for 700+.

In this book, the drills that follow each skill are also arranged easiest to hardest. Knowing the level of difficulty of a question is important. The easy questions are worth just as much as the hard ones. So, don't rush and risk a careless error just to reach the hard questions. If a question seems hard, take another look for what you are missing. Ask yourself, "Which skill can I use? What is the easy way to do this question?" After you complete this book, you will know!

Guessing? Don't randomly guess. But if you are unsure of a question, sometimes you can get it right with the process of elimination. When you can confidently eliminate at least one answer choice, take an educated guess. If you get it right, you gain four times as much as you lose if it's wrong. So educated guesses pay off. Of course, when you have completed this book, you'll rarely need to guess!

About Brian Leaf, M.A.

Six, maybe seven, people in the world know the SAT like Brian Leaf. Most are under surveillance in Princeton, NJ Brian alone is left to bring you this book.

Brian has seen the SAT from every angle, even teaching yoga to the test makers at ETS Corporation. You are about to find out what Brian learned from them while they slept in deep relaxation.

Brian is the author of *McGraw-Hill's Top 50 Skills* SAT and ACT test-prep series. He is also the author of *Defining Twilight: Vocabulary Workbook for Unlocking the SAT, ACT, GED, and SSAT* (Wiley, 2009). Brian is Director of the *New Leaf Learning Center* in Western Massachusetts. He teaches SAT, PSAT, and ACT prep to thousands of students from throughout the United States. (For more information, visit his website www.BrianLeaf.com.) Brian also works with the Georgetown University Office of Undergraduate Admissions as an Alumni Interviewer.

Acknowledgments

Special thanks to all the students of New Leaf Learning Center for allowing me to find this book. Thanks to my agent Linda Roghaar and my Editor at McGraw-Hill, Anya Kozorez. Thanks Pam Weber-Leaf for great editing tips, Larry Leaf for his one-liners, Zach Nelson for sage marketing advice, Ben Allison for his math genius, Matthew Thompson for astute design help, Susan and Manny Leaf for everything, and of course, thanks most of all to Gwen and Noah for time, love, support, and, in the case of Noah, hexagon finding and rejuvenating watermelon sandwiches.

Pretest

The following 50 questions correspond to our 50 Skills. Take the test, and then check your answers in the 50 Skill sections that follow.

Directions: This pretest contains the two types of math questions that you will see on the SAT: multiple-choice and student-produced response questions. Multiple-choice questions are followed by answer choices. Solve each and decide which is the best of the choices given. Student-produced response questions are not followed by answer choices.

You may use any available space for scratchwork. The use of a calculator is permitted.

❶ If m is a positive integer and $\frac{m+1}{3^2} = \frac{1}{3}$, what is the value of m ?

   Ⓐ -1

   Ⓑ 0

   Ⓒ 1

   Ⓓ 2

   Ⓔ 3

❸ If the average (arithmetic mean) of m and n is 7, what is $m + n$?

   Ⓐ 3.5

   Ⓑ 7

   Ⓒ 14

   Ⓓ 21

   Ⓔ 49

❷ If $4x + 2y = 12$, what is y in terms of x ?

   Ⓐ $6 + 2x$

   Ⓑ $6 - 2x$

   Ⓒ $12 - 4x$

   Ⓓ $12 - 2x$

   Ⓔ $x - 2$

❹ In the figure below, what is the value of a ?

   Ⓐ 25

   Ⓑ 30

   Ⓒ 35

   Ⓓ 40

   Ⓔ 45

⑤ In the figure below, if $a \parallel b$ and the measure of $x = 45$, what is the measure of y?

Ⓐ 27
Ⓑ 53
Ⓒ 127
Ⓓ 153
Ⓔ 163

⑥ If $MN = MO$ in the figure below, which of the following must be true?

Ⓐ $a = b$
Ⓑ $b = c$
Ⓒ $a = c$
Ⓓ $MN = NO$
Ⓔ $a = b = c$

Note: Figure not drawn to scale.

❼ In the figure below, what is the value of b?

Ⓐ 50
Ⓑ 55
Ⓒ 60
Ⓓ 65
Ⓔ 70

Note: Figure not drawn to scale.

(Question 8 is the first example in this book of an SAT student-produced response question, where you are not given multiple-choice options and must come up with your own answer.)

⑧ Let S equal the set of all real numbers. How many members of S are even prime numbers?

⑨ If P is the set of all <u>different</u>, real number, prime factors of 100, how many members does set P contain?

Ⓐ None
Ⓑ 2
Ⓒ 3
Ⓓ 8
Ⓔ 10

⑩ If x and y are positive integers, how many different ordered pairs satisfy the equation $x + y = 5$?

Ⓐ 0
Ⓑ 1
Ⓒ 2
Ⓓ 3
Ⓔ 4

⑪ If the slope of a line through the points (2, 4) and (0, b) is 1, what is the value of b ?

Ⓐ −2

Ⓑ −1

Ⓒ 0

Ⓓ 1

Ⓔ 2

⑫ In the xy coordinate plane, line j is the reflection of line k about the x axis. If the slope of line j is −3/4, what is the slope of line k ?

Ⓐ 4/3

Ⓑ 3/4

Ⓒ 1/4

Ⓓ −3/4

Ⓔ −4/3

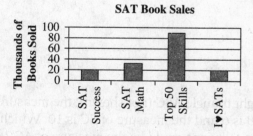

SAT Book Sales

⑬ According to the graph above, which two SAT books sold the fewest copies?

Ⓐ SAT Math and I♥SATs

Ⓑ I♥SATs and Top 50 Skills

Ⓒ I♥SATs and SAT Success

Ⓓ SAT Success and SAT Math

Ⓔ SAT Math and Top 50 Skills

⑭ If f(x) = 2x + 1, what is f(3) ?

⑮ If f(x) = 2x + 1 and f(m) = 9, what is m ?

⑯ Grandma Jones is making cookies for the fair. She needs x cups of flour per batch. Each batch makes c number of cookies. If she has 10 cups of flour, in terms of x and c, how many cookies can she make?

Ⓐ xc

Ⓑ 10xc

Ⓒ $\frac{10c}{x}$

Ⓓ $\frac{10x}{c}$

Ⓔ $\frac{xc}{10}$

⑰ In the figure above, the perimeter of square BCDF is 12, and the perimeter of rectangle ACEG is 30. If AB and DE are each positive integers, what is one possible value of the area of rectangle ACEG ?

18 In the diagram above, if the area of the large circle is 10 and the area of the small circle is 8, what is the area of the shaded region?

19 In a mixture of pretzels and corn chips, the ratio of pretzels to corn chips is 3 to 7. How many pretzels will be in a mixture that has 100 total pieces in it?

Ⓐ 70

Ⓑ 50

Ⓒ 37

Ⓓ 30

Ⓔ 4

20 If the numerator of a fraction is 3 more than the denominator, and the fraction equals $\frac{4}{3}$, what is the numerator of the fraction?

Ⓐ 3

Ⓑ 6

Ⓒ 9

Ⓓ 12

Ⓔ 18

21 In the figure below, *ABED* is a square with sides of length 6. If *EC* = 3, what is the perimeter of quadrilateral *ABCD* ?

Ⓐ 24

Ⓑ 27

Ⓒ $18 + 3\sqrt{5}$

Ⓓ $21 + 3\sqrt{5}$

Ⓔ $22 + \sqrt{47}$

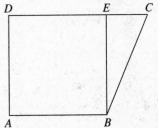

22 Points *A*, *B*, *C*, *D*, and *E* are collinear. If *B* is the midpoint of $\overline{AC}$, *C* is the midpoint of $\overline{AD}$, and *D* is the midpoint of $\overline{AE}$, which of the following is the longest segment?

Ⓐ $\overline{AB}$

Ⓑ $\overline{AD}$

Ⓒ $\overline{BC}$

Ⓓ $\overline{BD}$

Ⓔ $\overline{CE}$

Note: Figure not drawn to scale.

23 In right triangle *ABC* (not shown), the measure of *AB* is 6 and the measure of *BC* is 10. Which of the following could be the measure of *AC* ?

Ⓐ 3

Ⓑ 4

Ⓒ 6

Ⓓ 8

Ⓔ 10

If triangle *MNO* (not shown) is congruent to triangle *PQR* shown below, which of the following is the measure of longest side of triangle *MNO* ?

Ⓐ 3

Ⓑ $3\sqrt{3}$

Ⓒ 6

Ⓓ $6\sqrt{3}$

Ⓔ 12

 If triangle *MNO* (not shown) is similar to triangle *PQR* shown below, and has a shortest side with length 4.5, which of the following could be the measure of longest side of triangle *MNO* ?

Ⓐ 4.5

Ⓑ 6.5

Ⓒ 9

Ⓓ 12

Ⓔ 15

㉖ If 20 percent of 10 percent of a number is 24 less than half the number, what is the number?

㉗ If $x^2 - y^2 = 36$ and $x - y = 12$, what is the value of $x + y$?

㉘ If *m, n,* and *p* are positive integers and $3^m \cdot 3^n \cdot 3^p = 81$, then the greatest possible value for *p* is

Ⓐ 1

Ⓑ 2

Ⓒ 3

Ⓓ 4

Ⓔ 5

㉙ If $8m^2p^3 = m^5p$, what is *m* in terms of *p* ?

Ⓐ $p^{2/3}$

Ⓑ $2p^{2/3}$

Ⓒ $8p^{2/3}$

Ⓓ $2p^2$

Ⓔ $8p^{-2}$

㉚ If McLovin's lawn-mowing service charges $25 to come to a house and $0.50 for each bag of leaves that they remove, which of the following equations express McLovin's fees for a visit if he removes *x* bags of leaves?

Ⓐ $y = 25$

Ⓑ $y = 25x + 0.5$

Ⓒ $y = 0.5x$

Ⓓ $y = 0.5x + 25$

Ⓔ $y = 25x$

31 Fletch F. Fletch buys an ice cream sundae that contains one scoop of ice cream, one sauce, and either a cherry or pineapple wedge on top. He can choose chocolate, vanilla, strawberry, or banana ice cream; he can choose chocolate, caramel, or berry sauce; and he can choose either the cherry or the pineapple wedge for the top. How many different arrangements of these ingredients for Fletch's ice cream sundae are possible?

32 On a touch football team there are 5 kids who will be assigned to fill the 5 positions: 1 quarterback, 3 receivers, and 1 lineman. If only 3 kids can play quarterback or lineman, how many arrangements of the team are possible?

33 Of the 24 chocolates in a box, 10 are solid milk chocolate, 10 are solid dark chocolate, and 4 are cream-filled. If Noah randomly chooses a chocolate from the box, what is the probability that it will NOT be solid dark chocolate?

(A) $\frac{1}{12}$

(B) $\frac{1}{6}$

(C) $\frac{5}{12}$

(D) $\frac{7}{12}$

(E) $\frac{5}{6}$

34 The median of a set of 9 consecutive integers is 42. What is the greatest of these 9 numbers?

35 If the graph of $y = ax^2 + bx + c$ is shown below, then the value of ac could be

  I. Positive

  II. Negative

  III. 0

(A) I only

(B) II only

(C) I or II

(D) I or III

(E) I, II, or III

36 At New Leaf High School some students who do yoga also run cross-country, and no one who runs cross-country is on the fencing team. Which of the following must also be true of the students at New Leaf High School?

(A) No one fences.

(B) No one who does yoga is a fencer.

(C) More students run cross-country than do yoga.

(D) More students do yoga than fence.

(E) Some of the students who do yoga do not fence.

37 All the following numbers have remainder 3 when divided by 4 EXCEPT

(A) 7

(B) 15

(C) 22

(D) 23

(E) 31

38 Which of the following are solutions to $|n + 3| = 5$?

I. 2

II. -2

III. -8

(A) I only

(B) III only

(C) II and III

(D) I and III

(E) I, II, and III

39 If a sequence begins with the number 3 and each term that follows is found by adding 4, what is the sum of the first 5 terms?

40 A sequence begins with the number 5. The next term is found by adding 4, and the next is found by multiplying by -1. If this pattern of adding 4 and then multiplying by -1 is followed, what is the 26th term in the sequence?

(A) -9

(B) -5

(C) 5

(D) 9

(E) 26

41 If $f(x) = 3x^2$, which of the following expresses $f(2p)$?

(A) $6p$

(B) $6p^2$

(C) $12p$

(D) $12p^2$

(E) $24p^3$

42 For the equation $y = -3x^3 - 2$, when $x = 1$, what is the value of $-2y$?

43 If $0.5mno = 0$ and $4nop = 12$, then which of the following must be true?

(A) $nop = 12$
(B) $mno = -0.5$
(C) $p = 0$
(D) $m = 0$
(E) $no = 3$

45 Let the operation ζ be defined by $m\ \zeta\ n = mn + m$. What is the value of $-2\ \zeta\ 5$?

(A) -12
(B) -5
(C) 0
(D) 10
(E) 14

46 If y is directly proportional to x^3, and $y = 64$ when $x = 2$, what is x when $y = 216$?

44 The graph of $y = g(x)$ is shown above. Which of the following equations represents all the points of $g(x)$ shifted 1 unit to the left?

(A) $y = g(x) + 1$
(B) $y = g(x + 1)$
(C) $y = g(x - 1)$
(D) $y = g(x) - 1$
(E) $y = g(x)$

47 If y is inversely proportional to x and $y = 12$ when $x = 4$, what is the value of x when $y = 8$?

(A) 48
(B) 32
(C) 24
(D) 6
(E) 3

Movie	Votes
Superbad	♥ ♥ ♥ ♥ ♥
Borat	♥ ❜
Wedding Crashers	♥ ❜
Godfather	♥

♥ = 10 votes

48 The table above shows the results of a survey in which 90 high school students voted for their favorite movie. Each student received one vote. According to the graph, how many more students favored *Superbad* than favored *Borat*?

(A) 3

(B) 3.5

(C) 35

(D) 39.5

(E) 40

49 Ahmed is both the 7th tallest and 7th shortest student in class. If everyone is a different height, how many students total are in the class?

50 The night before the SAT you should

(A) eat 2 pounds of pasta for runner's endurance energy

(B) eat two whole live lobsters for omega-3 fatty acids

(C) have a huge pre-SAT party

(D) drill Pythagorean theorem until 2 a.m.

(E) relax and sleep well

Use the Answers

For 11 years you've been trained to solve math problems the long way. "No shortcuts!" Mrs. Nicholas always said. Mrs. Nicholas was the best math teacher that I ever had, and her advice was correct for math class. But the SAT is multiple-choice, and we can save time and energy by using the answers. Instead of completing a long process of algebraic manipulation, simply test the answer choices to see which one works. This strategy works best when there are **variables** in the question and **numbers** in the answer choices.

Let's look at the question from the Pretest:

1. If m is a positive integer and $\frac{m+1}{3^2} = \frac{1}{3}$, what is the value of m ?

   (A) 21   (B) 0   (C) 1   (D) 2   (E) 3

Solution: This question looks pretty tough to some students, but "Use the Answers" makes it EASY! Just plug each answer choice in for m to see which one makes the equation work. Choice A does not work because when we plug -1 in for m in the

equation, we get $\frac{-1+1}{3^2} = \frac{0}{9} = 0$ instead of $\frac{1}{3}$. Choice D is the only one that works,

since $\frac{2+1}{3^2} = \frac{3}{9} = \frac{1}{3}$.

Correct answer: D

SAT Math Mantra #1
When you see <u>variables</u> in the question and <u>numbers</u> in the answers,
"Use the Answers."

Use the Answers Drills

Easy

1 If $2x - 3 = 17$, then $x = ?$

(A) -1

(B) 0

(C) 10

(D) 22

(E) 31

2 For which of the following values of p will the value of $4p + 2$ be less than 15 ?

(A) 7

(B) 6

(C) 5

(D) 4

(E) 3

Medium

3 If j is a positive integer and $\frac{j+1}{2^3} = \frac{1}{2}$, what is the value of j ?

(A) -1

(B) 0

(C) 1

(D) 2

(E) 3

4 If $|3 - n| < 4$, which of the following is a possible value of n ?

(A) 9

(B) 8

(C) 7

(D) 6

(E) -1

5 What value of t would make $\sqrt{\frac{-2(t)}{3}} = 6$?

(A) -54

(B) -27

(C) 0

(D) 27

(E) 54

Hard

6 The cost, in dollars, of production for u units at Max's factory is expressed by the function $P(u) = 3500\left(\frac{6}{5}\right)^u$. If Max can spend \$7300 on production, what is the maximum number of units he can produce?

(A) 0

(B) 1

(C) 2

(D) 3

(E) 4

Algebraic Manipulation...
"What Is *p* in Terms of *f*?"

SAT Myth Busters

Myth: Algebraic manipulation was invented in the dungeons of medieval Europe, a brutal byzantine torture.

Fact: Algebraic manipulation was actually invented in the bathhouses of ancient Greece and was not used for torture until the mid-1900s.

Students often come into my office and say, "This question says, 'What is *m* in terms of *p* and *q*' and I have no idea what that means, so I skipped it." I love these, because they are so easy to teach and to gain points with. "What is *m* in terms of *p* and *q*" is just a fancy way of saying "solve for *m*" or "use algebra to get *m* alone." Whatever letter is after the "what is . . ." is the variable that you solve for. That's it, and every SAT has several of these questions!

Let's take a look at the Pretest:

2. If $4x + 2y = 12$, what is *y* in terms of *x*?

(A) $6 + 2x$ (B) $6 - 2x$ (C) $12 - 4x$ (D) $12 - 2x$ (E) $x - 2$

Solution: Just use algebra to get *y* alone.

$$4x + 2y = 12$$
$$\underline{-4x \qquad -4x} \qquad \text{subtract } 4x \text{ from both sides}$$
$$2y = 12 - 4x \qquad \text{divide both sides by 2}$$
$$y = 6 - 2x$$

Correct answer: B

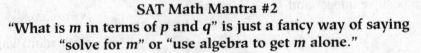

SAT Math Mantra #2
"What is *m* in terms of *p* and *q*" is just a fancy way of saying
"solve for *m*" or "use algebra to get *m* alone."

Algebraic Manipulation . . . "What Is p in Terms of f?" Drills

Easy

❶ If $D = RT$, what is R in terms of D and T ?

Ⓐ DT

Ⓑ $D - T$

Ⓒ $\dfrac{T}{D}$

Ⓓ $\dfrac{D}{T}$

Ⓔ $\dfrac{1}{DT}$

Medium

❷ If $3m = 2n$ and $2n = 4p$, what is m in terms of p ?

Ⓐ $\dfrac{3p}{4}$

Ⓑ $\dfrac{4p}{3}$

Ⓒ $12p$

Ⓓ $24p$

Ⓔ $10p^2$

Hard

❸ If $x + 3(b - 1) = k$, what is $b - 1$ in terms of x and k ?

Ⓐ $\dfrac{k}{3} - x$

Ⓑ $\dfrac{k - x}{3}$

Ⓒ $\dfrac{k + x}{3}$

Ⓓ $\dfrac{kx}{3}$

Ⓔ $\dfrac{k - 3}{x}$

❹ If p and q are positive and $5p^3q^{-2} = 25p^2$, what does p^{-1} equal in terms of q ?

Ⓐ $\dfrac{q^2}{5}$

Ⓑ $\dfrac{5}{q^2}$

Ⓒ $25q^2$

Ⓓ $5q^2$

Ⓔ $\dfrac{1}{5q^2}$

"Mean" Means Average

This is one of my favorite SAT strategies. It's true, I have favorite SAT strategies, but it's just such a good one and makes average questions so much easier.

The "average" of a list of numbers is found by adding them and dividing by how many there are.

$$\text{Average} = \frac{\text{sum}}{\text{number of items}}$$

This is very simple, and the SAT knows that you have been figuring out your grade point average, test average, or bowling average for years. Therefore, they do not usually ask you only to find the average of a list of numbers; they say, "Given the average, find the sum of the numbers." This gets kids, but if you know the strategy, it's easy! Just know this formula:

$$\text{Sum} = (\text{average}) \times (\text{number of items})$$

This is the key to unlock almost any average question on the SAT. As soon as you see the word "average" on the test, consider using this formula. By the way, anytime the SAT prints the word "average," they follow it with "(arithmetic mean)." This is simply a clarification and a synonym for "average." They are just referring to the normal average that you are used to, so ignore "(arithmetic mean)."

Let's look at the question from the Pretest:

3. If the average (arithmetic mean) of m and n is 7, what is $m + n$?

   (A) 3.5   (B) 7   (C) 14   (D) 21   (E) 49

Solution: For an average question, we use either the average formula or the sum formula. How do you know which? The question asks for one or the other! This question asks for the sum, so set up the sum formula:

Sum　　= (average) × (number of items)

$(m + n) =$　　7　　×　　2　　= 14

Correct answer: C

SAT Math Mantra #3
When you see the word "average" on the SAT,
use sum = (average) × (# of items).

"Mean" Means Average Drills

Medium

❶ If the average (arithmetic mean) of m and $4m$ is 30, what is the value of m ?

Ⓐ 4
Ⓑ 6
Ⓒ 8
Ⓓ 10
Ⓔ 12

❷ The average (arithmetic mean) of the scores of 21 students on an exam is k. In terms of k, what is the sum of the scores of all 21 students?

Ⓐ $21 + k$

Ⓑ $k - 21$

Ⓒ $\dfrac{k}{21}$

Ⓓ $\dfrac{21}{k}$

Ⓔ $21k$

❸ The average (arithmetic mean) of m and n is 7, and the average of m, n, and p is 11. What is the value of p ?

Ⓐ 31
Ⓑ 29
Ⓒ 21
Ⓓ 19
Ⓔ 15

❹ If the perimeters of two shapes have a sum of 9, what is the average (arithmetic mean) of the perimeters of the two shapes?

Ⓐ 0

Ⓑ $\dfrac{2}{9}$

Ⓒ $\dfrac{9}{4}$

Ⓓ $\dfrac{9}{2}$

Ⓔ 10

❺ The average (arithmetic mean) of the test scores of a class of 20 students is 80, and the average of the scores of a class of 30 students is 92. What is the average of both classes combined?

Ⓐ 25
Ⓑ 86
Ⓒ 87.2
Ⓓ 89.5
Ⓔ 92

❻ The average (arithmetic mean) of m, n, o, and p is 55. If the average of m, n, o, p, and q is 70, what is the value of q ?

Hard

❼ Each of 5 judges had a scorecard on which they wrote a different positive integer. If the average (arithmetic mean) of these integers is 7, what is the greatest possible integer that could be on one of the cards?

Skill 4

The Six-Minute Abs of Geometry: Angles

Every SAT has a bunch of geometry questions. Many students panic, "I don't remember the million stupid postulates we learned." Good news, you only need a small handful of those million postulates to solve most geometry questions.

Skills 4 through 7 show you how to find the measure of an angle in a diagram. Every SAT has several of these questions; memorize these skills and you will gain points, guaranteed.

❶ Vertical angles are equal. $a° = b°$

❷ The angles in a linear pair add up to 180°.

$m + n = 180°$

If you are given m, then $n = 180 - m$.

❸ The angles in a triangle add up to 180°.
The angles in a 4-sided shape add up to 360°.
The angles in a 5-sided shape add up to 540°.
The angles in a 6-sided shape add up to 720°.

$x + y + z = 180°$

Now, let's look at the question from the Pretest.

```
     100°
    /    \
  a°      140°
```

4. In the figure above, what is the value of a ?

(A) 25   (B) 30   (C) 35   (D) 40   (E) 45

Solution: This question uses two of our strategies: linear pair and 180° in a triangle. As soon as you see a linear pair of angles, determine the measures of the angles in the pair. So the angle next to the 140° must be 180° − 140° = 40°. Now we have two of three angles in a triangle which must add up to 180°, so the third must be 180° − 100° − 40° = 40°.

Correct answer: D

Math Mantra #4
**When you see vertical angles, a linear pair, or a triangle,
calculate the measures of all angles.**

Easy

❶ In the figure above, what is the value of *m* ?

Ⓐ 150

Ⓑ 80

Ⓒ 73

Ⓓ 27

Ⓔ 53

Note: Figure not drawn to scale.

❷ In the figure above, what is the value of *b* ?

Ⓐ 50

Ⓑ 55

Ⓒ 60

Ⓓ 65

Ⓔ 70

❸ If *y* = 60 and points *A*, *B*, and *C* lie on the same line, what is the value of *z* ?

Ⓐ 125

Ⓑ 100

Ⓒ 84

Ⓓ 62

Ⓔ 61

Medium

Note: Figure not drawn to scale.

❹ In the figure above, what is the value of *z* ?

Hard

❺ In the figure above, if *AB* is a line, what is *n* in terms of *m* ?

Ⓐ $180 - m$

Ⓑ $180 - 2m$

Ⓒ $\dfrac{180 - m}{2}$

Ⓓ $\dfrac{180 - m}{3}$

Ⓔ $\dfrac{180 - 2m}{3}$

The Six-Minute Abs of Geometry: Parallel Lines

In math class, learning about parallel lines can seem pretty tricky—alternate interior angles, corresponding angles, same-side interior angles. . . . We don't need all that for the SAT. We just need to know that

- Parallel lines are two lines that never touch.
- If two parallel lines are crossed by another line (called a transversal), then eight angles form.
- These eight angles are of two types, big or little. All bigs are equal, and all littles are equal.

This is enough to answer any parallel-lines SAT question. There's another 10 points!

Now, let's take a look at the question from the Pretest.

5. In the figure above, if $a \parallel b$ and the measure of $x = 45$, what is the measure of y ?

(A) 27   (B) 53   (C) 127   (D) 153   (E) 163

Solution: First, always mark any info from the question into the diagram, so mark $x = 45$. Remember SAT Math Mantra #4: when you are given two angles of a triangle, always determine the third: $180° - 108° - 45° = 27°$. Next, in the pair of parallel lines, there are only two kinds of angles, big and little. Angle y is big, not little, so it equals $180° - 27° = 153°$.

Correct answer: D

SAT Math Mantra #5
When you see two parallel lines that are crossed by another line,
eight angles are formed, and all the bigger-looking angles are equal,
and all the smaller-looking angles are equal.

The Six-Minute Abs of Geometry: Parallel Lines Drills

Easy

❶ In the figure below, $m \parallel n$. If $y = 45$, what is the value of x?

Ⓐ 45
Ⓑ 100
Ⓒ 135
Ⓓ 145
Ⓔ 180

❷ If $x = 66$ and $p \parallel q$ and $m \parallel n$ in the four lines shown, what is the value of z?

Ⓐ 24
Ⓑ 66
Ⓒ 90
Ⓓ 114
Ⓔ 166

❸ In the figure below, $m \parallel n$. If $z = 40$ and $x = 130$, then $y =$

Ⓐ 90
Ⓑ 80
Ⓒ 40
Ⓓ 50
Ⓔ 20

Note: Figure not drawn to scale.

Medium

❹ If $z = 45$ and $y = 95$ in the figure below, then which of the following must be true?

Ⓐ $p \parallel q$
Ⓑ $x + y = 180$
Ⓒ $z = x$
Ⓓ $x + z = 180$
Ⓔ $y = 2x$

Note: Figure not drawn to scale.

❺ In the figure below, if $a \parallel b$ and the measure of $x = 22$, what is the measure of y?

Ⓐ 22
Ⓑ 50
Ⓒ 90
Ⓓ 108
Ⓔ 130   Note: Figure not drawn to scale.

19

The Six-Minute Abs of Geometry: Triangles

Sir Bedevere: . . . and that, my liege, is how we know the Earth to be banana shaped.
King Arthur: This new learning amazes me, Sir Bedevere. Explain again how sheep's bladders may be employed to prevent earthquakes.

Monty Python and the Holy Grail (20th Century Fox, 1975)

Back in geometry class, you had a full chapter with 14 theorems classifying triangles. Here are two that matter for the SAT.

❶ If a triangle is isosceles (a fancy term for having two equal sides), then the two angles opposite the equal sides are also equal.

❷ If a triangle is equilateral (a fancy term for having all sides equal), then it has all equal angles of 60° each.

Let's take a look at the question from the Pretest.

Note: Figure not drawn to scale.

6. If MN = MO in the figure above, which of the following must be true?

(A) $a = b$ (B) $b = c$ (C) $a = c$ (D) $MN = NO$ (E) $a = b = c$

Solution: As soon as you are given info in the question, mark it in the diagram. This will remind you which geometry skill to use: since two sides are equal in the triangle, the two angles opposite the two sides are also equal. So $b = c$.

Correct answer: B

SAT Math Mantra #6
When you see a triangle with two equal sides, mark the two opposite angles as equal, and when all sides of a triangle are equal, mark all angles 60°.

The Six-Minute Abs of Geometry: Triangles Drills

Easy

❶ If triangle *EQU*, shown above, is equilateral, what is the value of *r* ?

Ⓐ 30
Ⓑ 60
Ⓒ 90
Ⓓ 120
Ⓔ 150

❷ If *MN* = *ON* in the figure above, and *b* = 43, what is the value of *c* ?

Ⓐ 43
Ⓑ 68.5
Ⓒ 75.5
Ⓓ 137
Ⓔ 153.5

Medium

Note: Figure not drawn to scale.

❸ If triangle *ABC*, shown above, has the perimeter of 21, and if *AC* = *AB* = 7, what is the value of ∠*ACB* ?

Ⓐ 7°
Ⓑ 14°
Ⓒ 30°
Ⓓ 60°
Ⓔ 90°

Note: Figure not drawn to scale.

❹ If the area of right triangle *MNO* is 72, and the measure of *MO* is 12, what is the value of ∠*MON* ?

Ⓐ 15°
Ⓑ 30°
Ⓒ 45°
Ⓓ 72°
Ⓔ 144°

The Final Six-Minute Abs of Geometry

By the end of this Skill, you will have learned all that you need to know about angles for the SAT. That's great news because **every** SAT includes several angle questions, and now you can always get them right. You know what to expect, you know what to use, and you will earn 30 or more points!

Here are the last two concepts for finding an angle:

❶ An exterior angle equals the sum of the two far away interior angles.

$$x = a + b$$

❷ "Bisect" means to cut into two equal parts. An angle bisector cuts an angle into two equal parts, and a segment bisector cuts a segment into two equal parts.

Segment *BD* bisects angle *ABC*. It cuts it into two equal parts, so $x = y$.

Point *P* bisects segment *MN*. It is the midpoint and cuts the segment into 2 equal parts, so $MP = PN$.

Now, let's take a look at the question from the Pretest.

Note: Figure not drawn to scale.

7. In the figure above, what is the value of *b*?

(A) 50   (B) 55   (C) 60   (D) 65   (E) 70

Solution: This is essentially a question from Skill 4, but this time we know the exterior angle trick. Since an exterior angle equals the sum of the two far away interior angles, $80 = 25 + b$. So $b = 55$.

Correct answer: B

SAT Math Mantra #7
An exterior angle equals the sum of the two far away interior angles.

The Final Six-Minute Abs of Geometry Drills

Medium

Note: Figure not drawn to scale.

❶ In the figure above, what is the value of $y - x$?

Note: Figure not drawn to scale.

❷ In the figure above, segments *AC* and *BD* intersect at *E*. If the measure of ∠*AEB* is 70° and segment *EF* (not shown) bisects ∠*BEC*, what is the measure of ∠*FED* ?

Hard

❸ In the figure above, if $x = 71$, what is the value of $y + z$?

- Ⓐ 71
- Ⓑ 142
- Ⓒ 211
- Ⓓ 251
- Ⓔ 282

❹ In the figure above, the dotted lines bisect angles with measures $x°$ and $y°$. In terms of x and y, what is the value of z ?

- Ⓐ $180 - 0.5(x + y)$
- Ⓑ $0.5(x + y)$
- Ⓒ $180 - (x + y)$
- Ⓓ $180 + (x - y)$
- Ⓔ $90 - 0.5(x - y)$

Math Vocab

Students come into my office and say, "I can't do this question because I don't know what 'consecutive' means." I get to say, "Oh cool, it just means numbers in a row, like 4, 5, 6." Then the question becomes easy. In fact, for some questions, the only hard part is knowing the vocabulary, and once you know the terms, the questions are easy. That's why I love this strategy; memorize these terms and practice using them in the drills, and you will absolutely gain points, guaranteed. Also, once you know the terms, watch for them and <u>underline</u> them when they appear. That will eliminate many careless errors.

Here are the first nine math vocabulary terms:

Real number—any number: $-3, -2.2, 0, \sqrt{2}, \pi$.

Constant term—this term really throws some kids, but it just means a letter in place of a number, kinda like a variable, except that it won't vary.

Integer—number without decimals or fractions: $-3, -2, -1, 0, 1, 2, 3, \ldots$. This is the single most common SAT math vocab word!

Even/odd—even numbers: $2, 4, 6, 8, \ldots$; odd numbers: $1, 3, 5, 7, \ldots$.

Positive/negative—positive numbers are greater than 0; negative numbers are less than 0.

Consecutive numbers—numbers in a row: 7, 8, 9, 10.

Different numbers—numbers that are . . . ummm . . . different.

Prime—a number whose only factors are 1 and itself. $2, 3, 5, 7, 11, 13, 17, \ldots$ are prime. Note: The number 1 is NOT considered prime, and the number 2 is the *only* even prime number.

Units digit—just a fancy term for the "ones" digit in a number, like the 2 in 672.

> Let's take a look at the question from the Pretest.
>
> 8. Let S equal the set of all real numbers. How many members of S are even prime numbers?

Solution: List the primes: 2, 3, 5, 7, 11, 13, 17, 19, 23. Only the number 2 is prime and even. No other primes can be even, since every even number (besides the number 2) has factors other than 1 and itself.

Correct answer: 1

SAT Math Mantra #8
Anytime you see a math vocab term, underline it.

Math Vocab Drills

Easy

1 If 2 consecutive integers have a sum of 9, what is the larger number?

2 How many different integers satisfy the equation $x^2 = 9$?

Ⓐ 0
Ⓑ 1
Ⓒ 2
Ⓓ 3
Ⓔ 4

3 How many positive integers less than 100 have a units digit of 3?

Ⓐ 100
Ⓑ 50
Ⓒ 33
Ⓓ 11
Ⓔ 10

Medium

4 If 2 consecutive prime numbers have a sum of 60, what is the larger number?

5 Two consecutive even integers have a sum of −26. Which of the following must be true?

  I. Both numbers are negative. ✗
  II. The lesser number is −12.
  III. The lesser number is −14.

Ⓐ I only. ✗
Ⓑ II only.
Ⓒ I and III only. ✓
Ⓓ II and III only.
Ⓔ I, II, and III. ✗

Hard

6 Let S equal the set of all positive integers less than 12. How many members of S are not consecutive odd prime numbers?

More Math Vocab

Here are three more math vocab terms. Memorize them, practice using them, and remember to underline them in questions. That will avoid heaps of careless errors.

Factors—numbers that divide into a number evenly (i.e., without a remainder).
Example: The factors of 48 are 1, 2, 3, 4, 6, 8, 12, 16, 24, 48.

1 2 3 4 6 8 12 16 24 48

When asked for the factors of a number, make a list of pairs like the ones shown above. This eliminates the possibility of missing any.

Prime factors—the factors of a number that are also prime numbers.
(Remember, a prime number is a number whose only factors are 1 and itself.)
Example: The prime factors of 48 are 2 and 3. These are the factors of 48 that also happen to be prime numbers.

Multiples—all the numbers that are divisible by a certain number.
Example: The multiples of 3 are 3, 6, 9, 12, 15, 18, 21, etc.

Now, let's take a look at the question from the Pretest.

9. If P is the set of all <u>different</u>, real number, prime factors of 100, how many members does set P contain?

(A) None   (B) 2   (C) 3   (D) 8   (E) 10

Solution: To complete this question, we factor 100 just as we factored 48 above.

1 2 4 5 10 20 25 50 100

Then we circle any prime numbers in the list. The numbers 2 and 5 are the only prime numbers in the list, so set P has 2 members.

Correct answer: B

SAT Math Mantra #9
Anytime you see a math vocab term, underline it.

More Math Vocab Drills

Brian's Math Magic Tricks
Trick #1—Multiples
Answer the following questions aloud.

What is 2 × 2 ?
What is 4 × 2 ?
What is 8 × 2 ?
What is 16 × 2 ?
What is 32 × 2 ?
What is 64 × 2 ?
Name a vegetable.

Turn to the solutions page to be amazed.

Easy

❶ Each of the following is a factor of 120 EXCEPT

Ⓐ 3
Ⓑ 4
Ⓒ 5
Ⓓ 6
Ⓔ 7

❷ Which of the following is an odd number that is a factor of 114 ?

Ⓐ 2
Ⓑ 13
Ⓒ 55
Ⓓ 57
Ⓔ 61

❸ How many integer factors does the number 48 have?

Ⓐ None
Ⓑ 1
Ⓒ 3
Ⓓ 8
Ⓔ 10

Medium

❹ If P is the set of all different, real number, prime factors of 48 that are also factors of 100, how many members does set P contain?

Ⓐ None
Ⓑ 1
Ⓒ 2
Ⓓ 3
Ⓔ 52

❺ What is the lowest number that is a multiple of 10, 12, and 15 ?

Ⓐ 1800
Ⓑ 900
Ⓒ 120
Ⓓ 60
Ⓔ 30

Hard

❻ If a, b, and c are different prime numbers, how many factors does ab^2c have?

Ⓐ 3
Ⓑ 5
Ⓒ 9
Ⓓ 10
Ⓔ 12

Fancy Math Vocab

Kids come into my office and say, "I skipped #10 because I never learned what an 'ordered pair' is." My job is easy. I get to say, "Yea, that's a funny thing. 'Ordered pair' is just a fancy term for a normal (x, y) point on a graph that you are used to; it's just a silly name. Don't be intimidated by it!" I love teaching vocabulary terms because they are such easy points to rack up. Know the vocab, and you'll get the question correct!

So, here are three fancy vocabulary terms:

xy coordinate plane—a fancy term for the normal grid that you graph lines on.

Cartesian plane—a fancy term for the normal grid that you graph lines on.

Ordered pair—a fancy term for a pair of coordinates (x, y) on the xy coordinate plane.

Now, let's take a look at the question from the Pretest.

10. If x and y are positive integers, how many different ordered pairs satisfy the equation $x + y = 5$?

(A) 0   (B) 1   (C) 2   (D) 3   (E) 4

Solution: Once you realize that "ordered pair" just means (x, y), it is easy. Just be systematic. Now x and y must be positive, so start with $x = 1$ (which is the lowest positive integer).

If $x = 1$, then $1 + y = 5$, so $y = 4$.   ordered pair: $(1, 4)$
If $x = 2$, then $2 + y = 5$, so $y = 3$.   ordered pair: $(2, 3)$
If $x = 3$, then $3 + y = 5$, so $y = 2$.   ordered pair: $(3, 2)$
If $x = 4$, then $4 + y = 5$, so $y = 1$.   ordered pair: $(4, 1)$
If $x = 5$, then $5 + y = 5$, so $y = 0$. This does not work since y must be positive and cannot equal 0, so we found all the solutions, and there are 4 ordered pairs.

Correct answer: E

SAT Math Mantra #10
Don't be intimidated by fancy vocabulary terms.

Fancy Math Vocab Drills

Medium

1 In an xy coordinate plane, if one circle is tangent to the x axis, and a different circle is tangent to the y axis, at how many ordered pairs (x, y) might the two circles intersect?

   I. 0

  II. 1

 III. 2

(A) I only

(B) II only

(C) I and III

(D) II and III

(E) I, II, and III

2 If x and y are positive integers, how many different ordered pairs satisfy the equation $x + y < 5$?

(A) 0

(B) 2

(C) 4

(D) 6

(E) 8

3 In the Cartesian plane, if the line with equation $y = 2x - b$ intersects the line defined by $y = ax + \frac{11}{2}$ at $(3, 4)$, what is the value of ab ?

(A) -1

(B) -2

(C) -4

(D) -8

(E) -16

4 In the xy coordinate plane below, which of the following points has coordinates (x, y) such that $x^2 = y + 5$?

(A) A

(B) B

(C) C

(D) D

(E) E

Hard

5 If x and y are integers, how many different ordered pairs satisfy the equation $|x| + |y| < 2$?

(A) 6

(B) 5

(C) 4

(D) 3

(E) 0

Green Circle, Black Diamond: Slaloming Slope I

Slope questions appear on every SAT. This topic could fill a college-level course, but the SAT tests only a few concepts.

Most importantly, to find the slope of two ordered pairs, use the *slope formula*:

$$\text{Slope} = \frac{y_1 - y_2}{x_1 - x_2}$$

You should also know these other groovy SAT slope facts:

- The slope of a line measures its steepness—the steeper the line, the bigger the slope.
- A line has a positive slope if it rises from left to right.
- A line has a negative slope if it falls from left to right.
- A horizontal line has a slope of 0.

Let's apply this on the question from the Pretest.

11. If the slope of a line through the points (2, 4) and (0, b) is 1, what is the value of b ?

(A) −2   (B) −1   (C) 0   (D) 1   (E) 2

Solution: Plug the two points into the slope equation.

$$\frac{y_1 - y_2}{x_1 - x_2} \Rightarrow \frac{4 - b}{2 - 0} \Rightarrow \frac{4 - b}{2} = 1$$

Once you have $\frac{4 - b}{2} = 1$, you can simply "Use the Answers" and try each answer choice to see which one makes the equation work. Skill Preview: As we will see in Skill 20, you could also cross-multiply to solve this equation.

Correct answer: E

SAT Math Mantra #11
The slope of a line measures its steepness; the steeper the line, the bigger the slope.

Easy

1 If the slope of a line through the points $(3, a)$ and $(-2, -4)$ is $\frac{3}{5}$, what is the value of a?

Ⓐ -2
Ⓑ -1
Ⓒ 0
Ⓓ 1
Ⓔ 2

2 What is the slope of the line through the point $(2, -3)$ and the origin?

Ⓐ -2.5
Ⓑ -1.5
Ⓒ -1
Ⓓ 0.5
Ⓔ 2.5

3 Which of the following is closest to the slope of the line in the figure below?

Ⓐ 0
Ⓑ $\frac{1}{4}$
Ⓒ $\frac{1}{2}$
Ⓓ 1
Ⓔ 2

Medium

4 In the figure below, the line containing (a, b) passes through the origin. What is the value of $\frac{b}{a}$?

Ⓐ -1
Ⓑ 0
Ⓒ 1
Ⓓ 3
Ⓔ Undefined

Hard

5 In the xy coordinate plane below, the indicated diameters of the two circles shown are parallel to the y axis. If the points M and N are centers of the circles, what is the slope of line MN (not shown)?

Ⓐ $\frac{2}{3}$
Ⓑ $\frac{2}{5}$
Ⓒ $\frac{3}{5}$
Ⓓ 1
Ⓔ 2

Green Circle, Black Diamond: Slaloming Slope II

Here are the rest of the slope rules on the SAT. You should memorize these; they are on **every** SAT!

- Parallel lines have equal slopes.
- Perpendicular lines have negative reciprocal slopes,

  Example: $\frac{2}{3}$ and $-\frac{3}{2}$

- Lines reflected over the x axis or y axis have negative slopes.

  Example: $\frac{2}{3}$ and $-\frac{2}{3}$.

  A reflection is like a mirror image. In the diagram to the right, line m is the reflection of line l over the x axis.

- Skill 30 preview: A line expressed in the form $y = ax + b$ has a slope of a. If the line is given in standard form $Ax + By = C$, use algebra to convert it to $y = ax + b$ form.

Let's take a look at the question from the Pretest.

12. In the xy coordinate plane, line j is the reflection of line k about the x axis. If the slope of line j is $-\frac{3}{4}$, what is the slope of line k ?

   (A) $\frac{4}{3}$ (B) $\frac{3}{4}$ (C) $\frac{1}{4}$ (D) $-\frac{3}{4}$ (E) $-\frac{4}{3}$

Solution: This question is quite difficult for most students. But with our strategies it's very easy. We know that two lines that are reflections of each other simply have the same slope but with opposite signs; so instead of $-\frac{3}{4}$, line j has a slope of $+\frac{3}{4}$.

Correct answer: B

SAT Math Mantra # 12

Parallel lines have equal slopes, like $\frac{2}{3}$ and $\frac{2}{3}$.

Perpendicular lines have negative reciprocal slopes, like $\frac{2}{3}$ and $-\frac{3}{2}$.

And lines reflected over the x axis or y axis have negative slopes, like $\frac{2}{3}$ and $-\frac{2}{3}$.

Green Circle, Black Diamond: Slaloming Slope II Drills

Medium

1 What is the slope of the line perpendicular to the line through the points (2, 3) and (−1, 0) ?

Ⓐ −1

Ⓑ 0

Ⓒ 1

Ⓓ 3

Ⓔ Undefined

2 If the line through the points (2, −3) and (4, p) is parallel to the line $y = -2x - 3$, what is the value of p ?

Ⓐ 7

Ⓑ 3

Ⓒ 0

Ⓓ −3

Ⓔ −7

3 What is the slope of the line perpendicular to the line through the point (2, −3) and the origin?

Ⓐ 0.4

Ⓑ $\frac{2}{3}$

Ⓒ 1

Ⓓ −2

Ⓔ 0.5

4 In the *xy* coordinate plane, line *n* is the reflection of line *m* about the *x* axis. If the slope of line *m* is $\frac{2}{3}$, what is the slope of line *n* ?

Ⓐ 1

Ⓑ −1

Ⓒ $\frac{2}{3}$

Ⓓ $-\frac{2}{3}$

Ⓔ $-\frac{3}{2}$

Hard

5 If the slope of a line through the points (2, 4) and (0, b) is 1, and the line through (b, 4) and (m, 6) is parallel to that line, what is the value of m ?

Ⓐ 0

Ⓑ 2

Ⓒ 4

Ⓓ 6

Ⓔ 8

The Sports Page: Using Tables and Graphs

Tables and graphs display information, just like the sports page lists a team's wins and losses. In fact, using tables and graphs should feel no different than checking stats for your favorite Red Sox pitcher, Halo III high scorer, or Guitar Hero hero.

SAT Math Mantra #13
The key to understanding tables and graphs is to read the headings and the legend, if there is one.

The SAT uses six kinds of tables and graphs. Tables display information in rows and columns. Usually the SAT asks you to use the last row or column, which shows totals. Pie graphs represent information as part of a pie. Line graphs display how data changes, often over time. Bar graphs compare the values of several items, such as sales of different toothpastes. Pictographs use small pictures to represent data. The key to pictographs lies in noticing the legend. If each icon represents 8 books, then $\frac{1}{2}$ of an icon represents 4 books, not $\frac{1}{2}$ of a book. Scatterplots compare two aspects of a group. When the SAT gives a scatterplot, it often asks you to name the equation of the line that best fits the data. Just sketch a line, estimate its y intercept and slope, and choose the equation (see Skill 30) that matches best.

Let's take a look at the question from the Pretest.

13. According to the graph above, which two SAT books sold the fewest copies?

   (A) SAT Math and I♥SATs
   (B) I♥SATs and Top 50 Skills
   (C) I♥SATs and SAT Success
   (D) SAT Success and SAT Math
   (E) SAT Math and Top 50 Skills

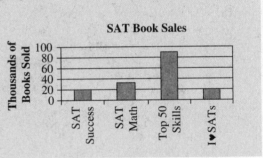

Solution: Obviously, Top 50 Skills is a stellar book and would sell the most, not the least copies, so that is out. According to the graph, SAT Success and I♥SATs sold the fewest copies.

Correct answer: C

The Sports Page: Using Tables and Graphs Drills

Easy

	Rookies	Veterans	Total
Yankees	a	b	c
Red Sox	d	e	f
Total	g	h	i

1 In the table above, each letter represents the number of home runs for that category. Which of the following must be equal to i ?

   I. $c + f$
  II. $a + b + d + e$
 III. $g + c$

(A) I only
(B) II only
(C) I and II
(D) II and III
(E) I, II, and III

Medium

Favorite Class Survey

2 The chart above shows the answers 500 people gave when asked to name their favorite teacher. Sra. Moran and Ms. Nicholas received the most votes. According to the graph, how many total votes were cast for these two teachers?

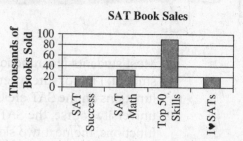

SAT Book Sales

3 According to the graph above, the four books averaged sales closest to

(A) 22
(B) 41
(C) 22,000
(D) 41,000
(E) 160,000

Test Results

4 The grid above shows the grades for students in Mr. Okin's history class on two tests. The x axis represents results on test I, and the y axis represents results on test II. Which student improved the most from test I to test II?

(A) A
(B) B
(C) C
(D) D
(E) E

The Only Function Questions on the SAT, Type I

Most students fear functions. "I suck at functions," I hear from almost every new student. I'm not sure where this attitude comes from, but here's the good news: functions on the SAT are easy. While functions could be the topic of a full-year university course, the SAT tests only two kinds of function questions. If you feared functions, the next two skills alone will earn you 3 more questions correct and raise your score 20 to 30 points!

Functions are just a type of equation, like $y = mx + b$. To show that an equation is a function, sometimes people replace the y with $f(x)$ or $g(x)$ or $h(x)$. That's it. Easy. To solve functions, remember that $f(x)$ is just a fancy way of saying y. So $f(x) = 2x - 1$ means the same as $y = 2x - 1$.

Now, let's look at the question from the Pretest.

14. If $f(x) = 2x + 1$, what is $f(3)$?

Solution: This is the first type of function question. This type simply asks you to plug the 3 in for x in the equation or graph. Cake! So $f(3) = 2(3) + 1 = 7$.

Correct answer: 7

Note: This type of function question might also ask you to use a graph instead of an equation to determine the answer. For example:

If the line shown in the graph below is $y = f(x)$, find $f(3)$. Based on the graph, $f(3) = 7$, since when $x = 3$, $y = 7$.

SAT Math Mantra #14
$f(3)$ means "plug 3 in for x."

The Only Function Questions on the SAT, Type I Drills

Easy

① If $f(x) = 2x^3 - 2$, what is the value of $f(-2)$?

Ⓐ -18

Ⓑ -16

Ⓒ -10

Ⓓ 8

Ⓔ 24

Medium

② For which of the following functions is $f(5) < f(-5)$?

Ⓐ $f(x) = 2x^2$

Ⓑ $f(x) = 2$

Ⓒ $f(x) = \dfrac{2}{x}$

Ⓓ $f(x) = 2 - x^3$

Ⓔ $f(x) = x^4 + 2$

x	f(x)
0	−1
1	2
2	11
3	26

③ The table above shows the values of the quadratic function f for selected values of x. Which of the following defines f ?

Ⓐ $f(x) = x^2 + 1$

Ⓑ $f(x) = x^2 + 2$

Ⓒ $f(x) = 3x^2 - 2$

Ⓓ $f(x) = 3x^2 - 1$

Ⓔ $f(x) = 3x^2 + 1$

④ The total weekly soap use, in pints, from washing x cars is given by the function $g(x) = 5x - (4x + k)$, where k is a constant. If last week 140 cars were washed, using 3 pints of soap, what is the value of k?

Ⓐ -137

Ⓑ -31

Ⓒ 1

Ⓓ 31

Ⓔ 137

⑤ If $m(n) = n^2 + 2n$ and $h(n) = 2n^2 - n$, then $m(6) - h(3) =$

Ⓐ 0

Ⓑ 15

Ⓒ 25

Ⓓ 33

Ⓔ 52

Hard

⑥ The graph of $y = f(x)$ is shown above. If $f(3) = m$, which of the following could be the value of $f(m)$?

Ⓐ $\dfrac{3}{5}$

Ⓑ 3

Ⓒ 0

Ⓓ -3

Ⓔ $-\dfrac{11}{3}$

Repeat after me, "I do not fear functions. I enjoy them. They are fun, easy, and interesting." As long as you don't get intimidated when you see the $f(x)$, functions are easy!

SAT Math Mantra #15

$f(m) = 9$ means "What did we plug into the equation for x to get a result of 9 ?"

Let's look at the question from the Pretest.

15. If $f(x) = 2x + 1$ and $f(m) = 9$, what is m ?

Solution: This is the second type of function question. It asks, "What did we plug into the equation for x to get a result of 9?" To solve, plug m in for x to get a result of 9, and solve for m:

$$9 = 2m + 1 \qquad \text{subtract 1 from both sides}$$
$$\underline{-1 \qquad -1}$$
$$\frac{8}{2} = \frac{2m}{2} \qquad \text{divide by 2}$$
$$\boxed{4 = m}$$

Correct answer: 4

Note: This type of function question might also ask you to use a graph instead of an equation to determine the answer. For example:

If the line shown in the graph below is $y = f(x)$, and if $f(p) = 9$, find p.

We need to find the x value on the graph below that corresponds to a y value of 9. An x value of 4 yields a y value of 9.

The Only Function Questions on the SAT, Type II Drills

Medium

❶ If $f(x) = 2x^2 - 3$, and $f(m) = -3$, what is the value of m ?

Ⓐ -3
Ⓑ -2
Ⓒ 0
Ⓓ 2
Ⓔ 3

❷ Let the function g be defined by $g(t) = 3(t^3 - 5)$. When $g(a) = -39$, what is the value of $4 - 2a$?

Ⓐ -31
Ⓑ -13
Ⓒ -8
Ⓓ 8
Ⓔ 13

❸ The graph of $y = f(x)$ is shown above. If $f(p) = 2$, which of the following is a possible value of p ?

Ⓐ -5
Ⓑ -4
Ⓒ 0
Ⓓ 2
Ⓔ 3

Hard

❹ If $m(n) = n^2 + n$ and $h(n) = n^2 - n$, which of the following is equivalent to $m(p - 1)$?

Ⓐ $h(p)$
Ⓑ $h(p) - 1$
Ⓒ $h(p) - 2$
Ⓓ $h(p) + 1$
Ⓔ $h(p) + 2$

❺ Let the function h be defined by $h(x) = x - 2$. If $3h(v) = 54$, what is the value of $h(2v)$?

❻ Let the function g be defined by $g(t) = t^2 - 3$. If m is a real number, how many possible values will make $g(3m) = 3g(m)$?

Make It Real

This is my single favorite SAT strategy. You're asking yourself, "What kind of dork has a favorite SAT strategy?" I do. Anyway, this strategy is amazing.

Let's take a look at the question from the Pretest.

16. Grandma Jones is making cookies for the fair. She needs x cups of flour per batch. Each batch makes c number of cookies. If she has 10 cups of flour, in terms of x and c, how many cookies can she make?

   (A) xc (B) $10xc$ (C) $\dfrac{10c}{x}$ (D) $\dfrac{10x}{c}$ (E) $\dfrac{xc}{10}$

Solution: You'd have to be Einstein to get this question; it's too theoretical. So we take it out of theory and "Make It Real." We choose real numbers in place of the variables, and it becomes totally easy. We can choose any numbers that seem to fit the equation, and we might as well choose numbers that work evenly and avoid decimals. For example,

- Let's say she needs 2 cups of flour per batch, so $x = 2$.
- Therefore, since she has 10 cups of flour, she can make 5 batches.
- Each batch produces c cookies. Let's say $c = 20$, so she can make 5 batches of 20 cookies. She can therefore make 100 cookies. EASY!

Now, we just go through the answer choices and plug our values for x and c into each. Whichever choice yields an answer of 100 is correct! So the answer is C, since

$$\frac{(10)(c)}{x} = \frac{(10)(20)}{2} = 100$$

Correct answer: C

This strategy turns very difficult questions into much easier ones!

SAT Math Mantra #16
When you see <u>variables</u> in the question and <u>variables</u> in the answer choices, especially for word problems, use "Make It Real."

Remember to try all answer choices. If more than one choice works for the values you choose, try a second set of values as a tie breaker.

Make It Real Drills

Easy

1 If p represents an even integer, which of the following expressions also represents an even integer?

Ⓐ $p - 3$
Ⓑ $2p - 1$
Ⓒ $2p - 2$
Ⓓ $3p + 1$
Ⓔ $4p + 3$

Medium

2 If x days ago Striped caterpillar was born and she is now n days older than her friend Yellow caterpillar, how old is Yellow in terms of x and n?

Ⓐ n
Ⓑ $x - n$
Ⓒ $n - x$
Ⓓ nx
Ⓔ $2x$

3 If p is a negative number, then $(5 \times 10^p) + (1 \times 10^p) =$

Ⓐ $\dfrac{5}{10}$
Ⓑ 60
Ⓒ $\dfrac{6}{10^{2p}}$
Ⓓ $\dfrac{6}{10^p}$
Ⓔ $6(10)^p$

4 A number q is multiplied by 7. The result is then added to 7. This result is then divided by 7. Which of the following expresses, in terms of q, the final result?

Ⓐ q
Ⓑ $q + 14$
Ⓒ $7q - 7$
Ⓓ $q + 1$
Ⓔ $q + 7$

Hard

5 If $-2 \leq m \leq 5$ and $-1 \leq n \leq 2$, what are all possible values of mn?

Ⓐ $mn = 4$
Ⓑ $2 \leq mn \leq 4$
Ⓒ $-2 \leq mn \leq 10$
Ⓓ $-4 \leq mn \leq 10$
Ⓔ $-5 \leq mn \leq 10$

6 If $-1 < n < 0$, which of the following expresses the correct ordering of n, n^2, and n^3?

Ⓐ $n < n^2 < n^3$
Ⓑ $n^2 < n < n^3$
Ⓒ $n < n^3 < n^2$
Ⓓ $n^3 < n < n^2$
Ⓔ $n^3 < n^2 < n$

7 If $m = \dfrac{3a^2}{v}$, what happens to the value of m when a and v are both doubled?

Ⓐ m is doubled
Ⓑ m is halved
Ⓒ m does not change
Ⓓ m is multiplied by 4
Ⓔ m is tripled

The SAT does not ask you to memorize any formulas. That's right, no memorizing. Actually, they do expect you to know perimeter formulas, but only a total jackass doesn't know these. I'm kidding; the perimeter of any shape is found by adding up the lengths of the sides. But any other formula that you need for area or volume is shown in the info box at the beginning of each math section. The box tells you:

Area of a triangle = $\frac{1}{2}$ (base)(height)

Area of a rectangle = (base)(height) = (length)(width)

Volume of a solid = (length)(width)(height)

Area of a circle = πr^2
Circumference of a circle = $2\pi r = \pi d$

For area and volume on the SAT, these are all the formulas that you'll need. Now, let's practice using them.

SAT Math Mantra #17
The SAT only expects you to use formulas provided in the question or in the info box at the beginning of the section.

Let's take a look at the question from the Pretest.

17. In the figure to the right, the perimeter of square *BCDF* is 12 and the perimeter of rectangle *ACEG* is 30. If *AB* and *DE* are each positive integers, what is one possible value of the area of rectangle *ACEG* ?

Solution: Since the perimeter of square *BCDF* is 12, each side must be 12 ÷ 4 = 3; and since the perimeter of rectangle *ACEG* is 30, *AB* + *DE* = 15 − 3 − 3 = 9. So *AB* and *DE* can be any 2 integers that add up to 9, for example, 1 and 8; and *AC* and *CE* would each be 3 units longer, 4 and 11. There are four such possibilities for the area of *ACEG*:

4 × 11 = 44, 5 × 10 = 50, 6 × 9 = 54, 7 × 8 = 56. Any one of these is a correct answer.

Correct answers: 44, 50, 54, or 56

Perimeter, Area, Volume Drills

1 If the square and the rectangle above have equal perimeters, what is the length of $\overline{RS}$?

(A) 5

(B) 6

(C) 8

(D) 10

(E) 16

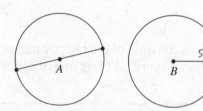

Note: Figure not drawn to scale.

2 For the circles above, the diameter of circle A is 10, and the radius of circle B is half the diameter of circle A. What is the area of circle B ?

(A) 5

(B) 25π

(C) 100π

(D) π

(E) 200π

Medium

3 The three-dimensional figure pictured above has square and triangular faces. If each square face has area m and each triangular face has area n, what is the total surface area of the figure in terms of m and n ?

(A) $m + n$

(B) $2(m + n)$

(C) $3m + 2n$

(D) $3m + 3n$

(E) $3mn$

4 The figure above shows the dimensions of a children's stacking block that is composed of rectangular solids. What is the volume of the block?

(A) 3

(B) 5

(C) 20

(D) 30

(E) 45

Donuts

OK, I lied in the previous Skill. There is one important formula that is not provided in the info box. To find the area of a shaded region, just subtract the area of the smaller figure from the area of the bigger figure. You might also be asked to find the perimeter of a shaded region.

Let's look at the question from the Pretest.

18. In the diagram above, if the area of the large circle is 10 and the area of the small circle is 8, what is the area of the shaded region?

Solution: The area of a shaded region is found by subtracting the little guy from the big guy. So $10 - 8 = 2$ and 2 is the area of the shaded region.

Correct answer: 2

An easy way to remember it: "The area of a donut equals the area of the big guy minus the area of the donut hole." This is a great formula. Almost every SAT has one question using it.

SAT Math Mantra #18
**The area of a donut equals the area of the big guy minus the
area of the donut hole.**

Donuts Drills

Medium

1 In the figure above, the perimeter of square *BCDF* is 24, *DE* = 4, and *AB* = 12. What is the area of the shaded region?

Ⓐ 204

Ⓑ 180

Ⓒ 144

Ⓓ 36

Ⓔ 24

3 In the figure above, what is the area of the shaded region?

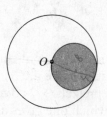

2 The small circle above is tangent to the large circle. If the radius of the large circle is 8, what is the area of the unshaded region?

Ⓐ 48π

Ⓑ 45π

Ⓒ 32π

Ⓓ 16π

Ⓔ 8π

Hard

4 In the figure above, triangles *ADB* and *EDC* are similar. If *AD* = 4, *ED* = 2, and *BD* = 6, what is the area of the shaded region?

Baking Granola Bars . . . Ratios

A ratio simply expresses a relationship between two numbers, such as: to bake granola bars, use 7 cups of oats to 2 cups of sugar. This can be written as 7 : 2 or $\frac{7}{2}$ or even 7 to 2. The SAT likes to see if you can play with the ratios. For example, if the ratio of boys to girls at Northampton High School is 5 to 6, then the ratio of girls to total students is 6 to 11. You have to be able to move between parts and the whole. Also remember that the numbers in a ratio may be reduced versions of the actual numbers. For example, if the ratio of boys to girls in a certain class is $\frac{2}{3}$, there might not actually be 2 boys and 3 girls, there might really be 4 boys and 6 girls. In this example $\frac{2}{3}$ is the reduced version and not the actual numbers: $\frac{2}{3} = \frac{4}{6}$.

SAT Math Mantra #19
4 boys to 5 girls could also be expressed 5 girls to 9 students.
Also a ratio can be a reduced version of the real numbers.

Let's look at the question from the Pretest.

19. In a mixture of pretzels and corn chips, the ratio of pretzels to corn chips is 3 to 7. How many pretzels will be in a mixture that has 100 total pieces?

(A) 70   (B) 50   (C) 37   (D) 30   (E) 4

Solution: This is a classic ratio question. You are given the ratio of pretzels to corn chips but are asked for the ratio of pretzels to total mixture. So switch the ratio. There are 3 pretzels per 7 corn chips, so there are 3 pretzels per 10 pieces total (3 pretzels + 7 corn chips = 10 delicious munchables). Now, just try the answers to see which one gives a ratio with 100 that is equal to 3 : 10. Choice D is correct since 30 : 100 equals 3 : 10. You could also solve this question by setting up a proportion and cross-multiplying, which we will discuss in the next Skill.

Correct answer: D

Baking Granola Bars . . . Ratios Drills

Easy

1 In a basket of whole vegetables, the ratio of carrots to potatoes is 2 to 7. Which of the following could NOT be the number of carrots in the basket?

Ⓐ 2
Ⓑ 3
Ⓒ 4
Ⓓ 10
Ⓔ 14

2 In a basket of apples and pears, 2 out of every 5 pieces of fruit are pears. Which of the following could be the number of apples in the basket?

Ⓐ 7
Ⓑ 14
Ⓒ 15
Ⓓ 22
Ⓔ 70

3 A 60-question test included 20 true/false questions. What fraction of the test was not true/false?

Medium

4 If the degree measures of the three angles in a triangle are in the ratio 1 : 3 : 5, what is the measure of the smallest angle?

Ⓐ 5°
Ⓑ 10°
Ⓒ 15°
Ⓓ 20°
Ⓔ 25°

5 If the degree measures of the three angles in a triangle are in the ratio 1 : 3 : 5, what is the difference between the measures of the largest and the smallest angles?

Ⓐ 70°
Ⓑ 80°
Ⓒ 90°
Ⓓ 100°
Ⓔ 110°

6 In a mixture of pretzels and corn chips, the ratio of pretzels to corn chips is 3 ounces of pretzels to 7 ounces of corn chips. How many ounces of pretzels will be in 16 ounces of the mixture?

More Granola Bars . . . Proportions and Cross-Multiplying

Two ratios that are equal are called a proportion. For example, $\frac{5}{12} = \frac{10}{24}$ is a proportion. If one of the four numbers in that proportion is unknown, cross-multiply to solve for it. For example, if $\frac{5}{12} = \frac{x}{40}$ and we want to find the value of x, just cross-multiply: $(5)(40) = (12)x$. Then use algebra to solve for x (divide both sides by 12 to get $x = 16.66$). Anytime the SAT shows you a proportion, they want you to cross-multiply. This is an exciting strategy. When you come to a proportion on the SAT, with our mantra, you will **always** get it right!

SAT Math Mantra #20
When you see a proportion on the SAT, cross-multiply.

Let's look at the question from the Pretest.

20. If the numerator of a fraction is 3 more than the denominator, and the fraction equals $\frac{4}{3}$, what is the numerator of the fraction?

    (A) 3   (B) 6   (C) 9   (D) 12   (E) 18

Solution: "Numerator" is just a super fancy word for the top of a fraction, and "denominator" is just the bottom. So if the numerator is 3 more than the denominator and the fraction equals $\frac{4}{3}$, we can represent this proportion as $\frac{d+3}{d} = \frac{4}{3}$ and cross-multiply to solve for d. $(d + 3)(3) = (d)(4)$, which equals $3d + 9 = 4d$. Collect like terms and $d = 9$. Notice that the question does not ask for d, but for the numerator, which is $d + 3$, so the numerator is 12. Always check to make sure that you've answered the question and didn't stop in a preliminary step. Skill 42 preview: Stopping too early is the most common SAT careless error that other students make.

Correct answer: D

More Granola Bars . . . Proportions and Cross-Multiplying Drills

Easy

1 According to Grandma Clara's recipe, 15 pounds of spelt flour is needed to make 50 cakes of dafillin. At this rate, how many pounds of flour is needed to make 1 cake?

- (A) 0.1
- (B) 0.2
- (C) 0.3
- (D) 1
- (E) 3

2 If $\frac{m}{12} = \frac{5}{n}$, what is the value of mn?

- (A) 60
- (B) 40
- (C) 30
- (D) 20
- (E) 14

3 If $\frac{m}{12} = \frac{3m}{n}$, what is the value of n?

- (A) 2.25
- (B) 4.5
- (C) 9
- (D) 18
- (E) 36

Medium

4 In a certain model airplane $\frac{1}{4}$ inch represents 4 feet. If the wing on the model is 1.5 inches, how long, in feet, is the wing on the actual plane?

- (A) $\frac{4}{5}$
- (B) 1
- (C) 18
- (D) 24
- (E) 36

Hard

5 If m, n, o, and p are all positive integers, all the following can be equivalent EXCEPT

- (A) $\frac{m}{n} = \frac{o}{p}$
- (B) $\frac{mp}{on} = 1$
- (C) $\frac{p}{n} = \frac{o}{m}$
- (D) $\frac{m}{p} = \frac{o}{n}$
- (E) $\frac{p}{o} = \frac{n}{m}$

Use the Diagram

Figures on the SAT are drawn perfectly to scale. I think they use lasers and fancy space-age machines to draw them—they're very accurate. Since they are so accurate, we can use the diagrams to estimate the answer to many questions. For a year in geometry class you were taught not to do this, and on the SAT it makes the question so much easier that it feels "cheap," like you are cheating. It's not! It's actually what they want you to do. Remember the test is supposed to test your cleverness, not what you learned in math class. This strategy brings out your innate cleverness.

Often in "Use the Diagram" we are given the length of some part of the diagram, and we use that to estimate the unknown. We've all done this before. Imagine you are on a road trip driving in a car. You look at the map and say, "We have to go from here to there on this squiggly highway." The map key says that each inch is 100 miles, so you use your thumb to represent an inch and you estimate the length of the squiggly line highway. That's the "Use the Diagram" strategy!

Sometimes "Use the Diagram" gives you the exact correct answer; at othertimes it is only a Plan B for when you can't figure out which of our geometry strategies to use.

Let's use this strategy on the question from the Pretest.

21. In the figure to the right, *ABED* is a square with sides of length 6. If *EC* = 3, what is the perimeter of quadrilateral *ABCD* ?

   (A) 24
   (B) $18 + 3\sqrt{5}$
   (C) 27
   (D) $21 + 3\sqrt{5}$
   (E) $22 + \sqrt{47}$

Solution: *AB*, *AD*, and *DE* are 6 and *EC* is 3, so we have a perimeter of least 21 so far. We can use the Pythagorean theorem to get *BC*. We can also "Use the Diagram." Clearly *CB* is slightly longer than *EB*, so slightly longer than 6, let's say 6.5. Thus, the perimeter is approximately $6 + 6 + 6 + 3 + 6.5 \approx 27.5$. Now try the answers. Use your calculator to translate $3\sqrt{5}$ and $\sqrt{47}$ into decimals: $-3\sqrt{5} = 6.6$ and $\sqrt{47} = 6.85$, — and see which answer matches. Choice D is correct.

Correct answer: D

SAT Math Mantra #21
"Use the Diagram" to estimate an answer.
Translate into decimals any answer choices that contain $\sqrt{\ }$ or π.

Use the Diagram Drills

Easy

M   N   O

❶ In the figure above, $MO = 12$ and $MN = NO$. Point A (not shown) is on the line between N and O such that $NA = AO$. What does MA equal?

(A) 6

(B) 9

(C) 12

(D) 15

(E) 18

Medium

❷ The rectangular solid above has edges of length 10, 4, and 2. If point M (not shown) is the midpoint of segment AB, what is the length of MC ?

(A) $\sqrt{10}$

(B) $\sqrt{17}$

(C) $\sqrt{26}$

(D) $\sqrt{35}$

(E) $\sqrt{41}$

❸ The small circle above is tangent to the large circle. If the radius of the large circle is 6, what is the perimeter of the unshaded region?

(A) 18π

(B) 15π

(C) 12π

(D) 8π

(E) 6π

Hard

J   K

L   M

❹ In the figure above, the measures of all five line segments are equal. What is the ratio of the length of $\overline{LK}$ to the length of $\overline{JM}$ (not shown)?

(A) $\dfrac{\sqrt{3}}{3}$

(B) $\dfrac{\sqrt{6}}{3}$

(C) $\sqrt{2}$

(D) $\dfrac{3\sqrt{3}}{3}$

(E) $3\sqrt{2}$

Here's your chance to relive your sixth-grade art class memories. We love the "Use the Diagram" strategy, but can we use it for diagrams that specifically say, "Note: Figure not drawn to scale"? What are we to do? Are we lost? NO! These questions are even easier. Simply resketch the picture somewhat accurately and then "Use the Diagram." It turns out that often the whole question is hinged on it being out of scale; when you put it into scale, the answer becomes obvious.

Also, while we're in art class here's another great strategy. If a question describes a diagram, but none is shown, draw one. Sometimes this gives the answer immediately, and at othertimes it shows you what to do next, but either way it always helps!

SAT Math Mantra #22
When a diagram is not drawn to scale, redraw it.
And when a picture is described but not shown, draw it!

Let's look at the Pretest question.

Note: Figure not drawn to scale.

22. Points A, B, C, D, and E are collinear. If B is the midpoint of $\overline{AC}$, C is the midpoint of $\overline{AD}$, and D is the midpoint of $\overline{AE}$, which of the following is the longest segment?

   (A) $\overline{AB}$ (B) $\overline{AD}$ (C) $\overline{BC}$ (D) $\overline{BD}$ (E) $\overline{CE}$

Solution: Simply redraw the diagram to scale, following the instructions in the question:

A   B   C   D   E

Then the answer is obvious. Of the choices, $\overline{CE}$ is longest.

Correct answer: E

Art Class Drills

Easy

1 If points *L*, *M*, *N* and *O* are collinear, *LM* = *MO* = 12, and *N* is between *M* and *O*, which of the following could be the measure of segment *LN* ?

Ⓐ 4
Ⓑ 8
Ⓒ 12
Ⓓ 15
Ⓔ 24

Medium

2 In an *xy* coordinate plane (not shown) three points *Q*, *R*, and *S* have coordinates (2, 7), (2, 3), and (5, *b*). If the three points determine a right triangle, what is one possible value of *b* ?

3 If the sides of quadrilateral *ACEG* below are all equal, and ∠*AGE* = 90°, what is the ratio of *AE* to *CE* ?

Note: Figure not drawn to scale.

Ⓐ 3 to 1
Ⓑ 2 to 1
Ⓒ $\sqrt{2}$ to 1
Ⓓ $\sqrt{2}$ to 2
Ⓔ $\sqrt{2}$ to $\sqrt{3}$

4 A cube has edges of length 2. If point *M* is the midpoint of edge *AB*, what is the length of the segment from point *M* to the center of the cube?

Ⓐ $\sqrt{2}$
Ⓑ $\sqrt{3}$
Ⓒ $2\sqrt{2}$
Ⓓ $2\sqrt{3}$
Ⓔ 6

Note: Figure not drawn to scale.

5 In the figure above, segments *MN* and *JK* are each perpendicular to *JM*. If *x* = 30, the measure of *LN* is 12, and the measure of *KL* is 4, what is the measure of *JM* ?

Ⓐ $3\sqrt{3}$ (approximately 5.19)
Ⓑ $5\sqrt{3}$ (approximately 8.66)
Ⓒ $6\sqrt{3}$ (approximately 10.39)
Ⓓ $8\sqrt{3}$ (approximately 12.12)
Ⓔ $10\sqrt{3}$ (approximately 13.86)

The Six-Minute Abs of Geometry: Length of a Side I

In Skills 4–7, we looked at finding missing angles in a diagram. Skills 23–25 show you how to find a missing side in a diagram. **You do not need to memorize these formulas; they are provided in the information box at the beginning of every math section.**

I come from a long line of teachers. My grandfather, Herman, was a beloved teacher and principal in Zshmolphf, Austria (mostly true). His father was a scholar (true). His father's father was a scholar. Some say we can trace our lineage back thousands of years to the James Brown of geometry, the godfather of good math, your friend and mine, the mighty Pythagoras (lie), best known for his theorem $a^2 + b^2 = c^2$. Pythagoras is also definitely a favorite of the folks at the SAT. His theorem is used on EVERY SAT.

Use the Pythagorean theorem, $a^2 + b^2 = c^2$, to find the length of a side of a right triangle when you are given the lengths of the other two. As I said, this is used on EVERY SAT. In fact, anytime you see a right triangle on the SAT, you will probably need it. Just fill the two sides that you know into the equation, and solve for the third. Here's an example:

If $a = 6$ and $c = 10$, what is the value of b?

$$a^2 + b^2 = c^2$$
$$6^2 + b^2 = 10^2$$
$$36 + b^2 = 100$$
$$b^2 = 64$$
$$b = 8$$

SAT Math Mantra #23
When you see a right triangle, try $a^2 + b^2 = c^2$.

Let's use good ol' Pythagoras on the question from the Pretest.

23. In right triangle *ABC* (not shown), the measure of *AB* is 6 and the measure of *BC* is 10. Which of the following could be the measure of *AC* ?

    (A) 3   (B) 4   (C) 6   (D) 8   (E) 10

Solution: Great review of SAT Math Mantra #22, "When a picture is described but not shown, draw it." This helps you visualize and organize the info and shows you what to do next. The question does not state whether 10 is another short side like 6 or whether it is the longest side. But we can "Use the Answers" and simply try each answer choice in $a^2 + b^2 = c^2$, always using the biggest number for *c*. Choice A is not correct since $3^2 + 6^2 \neq 10^2$, and choice B is not correct since $4^2 + 6^2 \neq 10^2$, and so on. Choice D is correct since $6^2 + 8^2 = 10^2$.

Correct answer: D

The Six-Minute Abs of Geometry: Length of a Side I Drills

Easy

1 In the right triangle above, if $m = 5$ and $n = 12$, find the value of o.

Ⓐ 5
Ⓑ 12
Ⓒ 13
Ⓓ 15
Ⓔ 21

Note: Figure not drawn to scale.

2 If the figure above is a right triangle, what is the value of p?

Medium

3 In right triangle ABC (not shown), the measure of AB is 4 and the measure of BC is 10. Which of the following could be the measure of AC?

Ⓐ $2\sqrt{19}$
Ⓑ $2\sqrt{21}$
Ⓒ $2\sqrt{25}$
Ⓓ 84
Ⓔ 96

Hard

4 In an xy coordinate plane (not shown), three points Q, R, and S have coordinates (2, 3), (7, 3), and (2, m), respectively. If the three points determine a right triangle, with a hypotenuse of 13, and m is a positive integer, what is the value of m?

5 The lengths of the sides of a right triangle are consecutive integers, and the length of the longest side is x. Which of the following could be used to solve for x?

Ⓐ $(x - 2)^2 + (x - 1)^2 = x^2$
Ⓑ $x + x - 3 = x$
Ⓒ $(x - 2)(x - 1) = x^2$
Ⓓ $(x - 2) - (x - 1) = x$
Ⓔ $(x - 4)^2 + (x - 2)^2 = x^2$

The Six-Minute Abs of Geometry: Length of a Side II

When the Pythagorean theorem is not enough to find the length of a missing side, use one or both of the two "special right triangles."

❶ When the three angles of a triangle measure 30°, 60°, 90°, then the sides are x, $x\sqrt{3}$, and $2x$.

❷ When the three angles measure 45°, 45°, 90° (also called an isosceles right triangle), then the two short sides are equal, let's call them x, and the longest side measures $x\sqrt{2}$. Or, if you are given the long side, then the two short sides each measure $\frac{x}{\sqrt{2}}$.

SAT Math Mantra #24
When you see a 30°, 45°, or 60° angle in a right triangle, try using the special right triangles.

Now, let's use these on the question from the Pretest.

24. If triangle *MNO* (not shown) is congruent to triangle *PQR* shown below, which of the following is the measure of longest side of triangle *MNO* ?

(A) 3
(B) $3\sqrt{3}$
(C) 6
(D) $6\sqrt{3}$
(E) 12

Solution: When you see a right triangle on the SAT, first try the Pythagorean theorem. Given only one side of the triangle, we don't have much info to use in the Pythagorean theorem, so try the special right triangles. **Also the 60° angle is a clue to use special right triangles. When you see a 60° angle, try special right triangles.** Since there is a 90° and a 60° angle, the third angle must be 30°, so it is a 30, 60, 90 triangle and follows the pattern x, $x\sqrt{3}$, and $2x$ for the three sides. (You do not need to memorize these; they are provided in the information box at the beginning at of every math section.) Therefore, $PR = 3$ and the longest side of *PQR* equals 6. Since the two triangles are congruent, the measure of the longest side of *MNO* must also be 6.

Correct answer: C

The Six-Minute Abs of Geometry: Length of a Side II Drills

Medium

1 In right triangle *MNO* (not shown), the measure of *MN* is 8 and the measure of *NO* is 4. Which of the following could be the measure of *OM* ?

   I. 4

   II. $4\sqrt{3}$

  III. 2

   Ⓐ II only ✓

   Ⓑ III only

   Ⓒ I and II ✓

   Ⓓ II and III ✓

   Ⓔ I, II, and III ✓

Note: Figure not drawn to scale.

2 What is the length of the shortest leg of a triangle congruent to the triangle shown above?

   Ⓐ 3

   Ⓑ $3\sqrt{3}$

   Ⓒ 6

   Ⓓ $6\sqrt{3}$

   Ⓔ 12

Hard

3 In an isosceles right triangle, the sum of measures of the two equal sides is 6. What is the measure of the longest side?

   Ⓐ 3

   Ⓑ $3\sqrt{2}$ (approximately 4.24)

   Ⓒ 6

   Ⓓ $3\sqrt{3}$ (approximately 5.19)

   Ⓔ $6\sqrt{3}$ (approximately 10.39)

(Question 4 is very similar to a question you've seen before. See if you can solve it this time using special right triangles.)

Note: Figure not drawn to scale.

4 In the figure above, segments *MN* and *JK* are each perpendicular to *JM*. If *x* = 30, the measure of *LN* is 10, and the measure of *KL* is 6, what is the measure of *JM* ?

   Ⓐ $3\sqrt{3}$ (approximately 5.19)

   Ⓑ $5\sqrt{3}$ (approximately 8.66)

   Ⓒ $6\sqrt{3}$ (approximately 10.39)

   Ⓓ $8\sqrt{3}$ (approximately 12.12)

   Ⓔ $10\sqrt{3}$ (approximately 13.86)

The Six-Minute Abs of Geometry: Length of a Side III

> I shall call him . . . Mini-Me.
> Dr. Evil, *Austin Powers: The Spy Who Shagged Me* (New Line Cinema, 1999)

Similar triangles are two triangles where one is a shrinky version of the other, like Dr. Evil and Mini-Me. Since one is a shrunken version of the other, all sides are proportional.

Let's have a look at the question from the Pretest.

25. If triangle *MNO* (not shown) is similar to triangle *PQR* shown below and has a shortest side with length 4.5, which of the following could be the measure of longest side of triangle *MNO* ?

(A) 4.5
(B) 6.5
(C) 9
(D) 12
(E) 15

Solution: Here's your chance to see if you really learned Skill 24. We have to determine the measures of sides of triangle *PQR* shown above. Once you have the lengths of the sides of $\triangle PQR$, you can determine the lengths of $\triangle MNO$. Triangle *MNO* is "similar" to *PQR*, which means that the sides are proportional. So the ratio of the smallest sides must equal the ratio of the largest sides. Fill in the numbers and cross-multiply to solve. (Remember Mantra #20, "When you see a proportion, cross-multiply.")

$$\frac{\text{Smallest}}{\text{Smallest}} = \frac{\text{largest}}{\text{largest}} \Rightarrow \frac{3}{4.5} = \frac{6}{x}$$

So $3x = 27$ and $x = 9$.

Correct answer: C

SAT Math Mantra #25
Similar triangles have sides that are proportional.

The Six-Minute Abs of Geometry: Length of a Side III Drills

Medium

1 Isosceles triangle ABC is similar to triangle MNO above. If $AC = 3$, $AB = 4$, and $NO = 6$, what is the measure of MO ?

Ⓐ 3

Ⓑ 4.5

Ⓒ 6

Ⓓ 7.5

Ⓔ 9

2 If triangle MNO (not shown) is similar to triangle PQR shown above, which of the following could be the measures of the three sides of triangle MNO ?

Ⓐ $3\sqrt{3}$, $6\sqrt{3}$, 9

Ⓑ 6, $6\sqrt{3}$, 12

Ⓒ 6, 6, 12

Ⓓ $3\sqrt{3}$, $6\sqrt{3}$, 6

Ⓔ 12, 12, 6

3 The triangle pictured above is similar to triangle PRQ (not shown). If the ratio of the shortest side of the pictured triangle to the shortest side in triangle PQR is 2, what is the perimeter of triangle PQR ?

Ⓐ 1.5

Ⓑ 4

Ⓒ 5

Ⓓ 6

Ⓔ 12

4 The lengths of the sides of two similar triangles (not shown) have a ratio of 3 : 5. The lengths of the larger triangle are 4, 5, and 6. If x represents the measure of the shortest side of the smaller triangle, which of the following could be used to find x ?

Ⓐ $\dfrac{3}{5} = \dfrac{3}{x}$

Ⓑ $\dfrac{3}{5} = \dfrac{4}{x}$

Ⓒ $\dfrac{3}{4} = \dfrac{4}{x}$

Ⓓ $\dfrac{3}{5} = \dfrac{x}{4}$

Ⓔ $\dfrac{3}{4} = \dfrac{4}{x}$

The SAT is a marathon, and you must pace yourself and manage your energy. It serves you to focus and try your absolute hardest. It does not serve you to tense your face as you work, to clench your butt, or to shake your foot. You can focus and give your all without getting an ulcer, and best of all, you can spend less energy and do better on the test. You can be like a warrior, a ninja, a Jedi.

Here is a great yoga posture to practice using muscles that need to be used, but keeping all else relaxed. Record the following sequence onto your iPod, and then get yoga-ing. If you can't read the word "buttocks" without giggling, you can download the sequence as a free podcast from my website: www.BrianLeaf.com.

Stand up with your feet shoulder-width apart and parallel to each other (see Skill 5 if you don't remember the word "parallel"). Press the crown of your head up toward the ceiling—chin parallel to the ground. Beginning with your arms at your sides, inhale as you slowly raise your arms up overhead (as though flapping wings) and exhale as you slowly lower them. Repeat this 4 more times, slowly moving your arms up and down, coordinating your breath with the movement. . . . Then next time your arms are overhead, hold them there. Press your feet into the ground. Press your crown up toward the ceiling—chin parallel to the floor. Press your fingertips up toward the ceiling, simultaneously relaxing your shoulders. And breathe deep, slow breaths. Hold this posture for 10 breaths. As you hold the posture, notice where you are straining. See if you can relax. Your muscles are working to hold your arms up, but your face, feet, buttocks, and legs can be relaxed. Soften your facial muscles. Relax your belly, relax your feet and your neck. Practice being focused and alert, giving your all to the task, and yet being relaxed and soft. Being relaxed frees up more energy for the task at hand and improves your performance, while simultaneously reducing strain and stress, a pretty good tradeoff. It conserves energy and increases endurance.

Now, slowly lower your arms as you exhale. Then close your eyes and tune in to how you feel. Notice your muscles. Where do you feel strain? Now that they are no longer working to keep your arms up, see if you can allow your shoulders, back, and neck to relax and soften. Breathe a few deep breaths. Allowing your muscles to relax even more with each breath. . . . Then open your eyes and return to SAT prep relaxed, renewed, and ready to absorb new knowledge.

Set the intention to notice your muscles as you go about your day. Notice when muscles that need not be activated are tense, such as clenching a fist during SAT prep, and allow them to relax, unclench, and soften. This will reduce your stress, increase your endurance, and boost your performance. It will even allow you to retain more as you learn! You are a SAT ninja.

Guided Relaxation

Record the following sequence onto your iPod. Then lie back and let go. If you can't read it without giggling, you can download the sequence as a free podcast from my website: www.BrianLeaf.com.

Lie down on your back and close your eyes.

Take slow, deep breaths. Bring your awareness to your feet. Allow your feet to relax, like a fist unclenching.

Bring your awareness to your calves and shins. Let the muscles relax and soften and unclench.

Bring your awareness to your thighs and hips. Allow the thighs and hips to relax and unclench.

Bring your awareness to your whole legs. Allow the legs to relax even more, to soften even more. Allow all the muscles to drop, allow yourself to be fully supported by the floor.

Now, bring your awareness to your pelvis. Allow your pelvis to relax, to unclench and to drop and be supported by the floor.

Bring your awareness to your lower back. Allow your lower back to relax and drop.

Bring your awareness to your belly. Allow your belly to relax, to unclench, to let go.

Bring your awareness to your upper back and chest. Allow your upper back and chest to relax, to unclench. . . .

Bring your awareness to your neck, the front, sides, and back. Allow your neck to relax, to unclench, and to soften. . . .

Bring your awareness to your face: eyes, nose, mouth, and cheeks. Allow your face to soften, to relax, to unclench. . . .

Bring your awareness to your scalp. Allow your scalp to relax.

Now bring your attention to your whole body: feet, legs, pelvis, belly, back, chest, neck, head. Allow all your muscles to relax even more, to unclench even more. Allow all your muscles to soften and drop even more, allowing your whole body to be supported by the floor. . . .

Now relax a few minutes.

(Let 2 minutes pass on the recording. You can sample relaxing music here, probably not DMX.)

Now, gently begin to deepen the breath.

Breathe slow, deep breaths.

Wiggle the fingers and toes.

Slowly roll over to your right side and open your eyes.

Slowly sit up and make the intention to bring this feeling of relaxation and calm into all your activities: school, math homework, socializing, eating, sleeping, and of course SAT prep.

"Is" Means Equals . . . Translation

I love translation questions. It's like you are translating Spanish to English. On the SAT we are translating English to math and here is our dictionary:

"what number"	means	x
"37 percent"	means	0.37
"of" and "product"	mean	multiply
"less"	means	minus
"sum" or "more than"	means	plus
"quotient"	means	divide
"is"	means	equals
"is to" or "per"	means	divide (ratio) and often a proportion
"twice a number"	means	$2x$

Simply translate, word for word.

Here's the question from the Pretest.

26. If 20 percent of 10 percent of a number is 24 less than half the number, what is the number?

Solution: First translate. Then use algebra to solve.

$(0.20)(0.10)(n) = 0.5n - 24$	translate
$0.02n = 0.5n - 24$	multiply $(0.20)(0.10)$
$24 = 0.48n$	add 24 to both sides, and subtract $0.02n$ from both sides
$50 = n$	divide both sides by 0.48

Correct answer: 50

SAT Math Mantra #26
Translate word problems from English to math.

Let's try it, come along children. . . .

"Is" Means Equals . . . Translation Drills

Easy

> The product of b and 2 is equal to the sum of b and $\frac{2}{3}$.

❶ Which of the following is an expression for the relationship described above?

(A) $b - 2 = b + \frac{2}{3}$

(B) $b - 2 = \frac{2}{3}b$

(C) $2b = b + \frac{2}{3}$

(D) $2b = b - \frac{2}{3}$

(E) $4b = \frac{2}{3}$

Medium

❷ How many inches are there in f feet and c inches?

(A) $12(f + c)$

(B) $12f + c$

(C) $f + \frac{c}{12}$

(D) $\frac{f + c}{12}$

(E) $f + 12c$

❸ When the number p is added to 6, the result is the same as when p is multiplied by 5. What is the value of $8p$?

(A) $\frac{5}{6}$

(B) 3

(C) 8

(D) 12

(E) 14

Hard

❹ If $2x + 3y$ is equal to 120 percent of $5y$, what is the value of $\frac{y}{x}$?

❺ If the square of $(m + 11)$ equals the product of $(m + 1)^2$ and 9, what is the value of m ?

(A) 0

(B) 1

(C) 2

(D) 3

(E) 4

Just Do It! . . .
Springboard

When approaching a question, students often say, "I have no idea where to start!" This book, and this strategy especially, tells you where to start.

SAT Math Mantra #27
When something can be factored, FOILed, reduced, or simplified, . . . do it.

Examples:

- When you see $x^2 - y^2$, **factor** it to $(x - y)(x + y)$.
  Note: $x^2 - y^2 = (x - y)(x + y)$ is the SAT's favorite kind of factoring. Memorize it!
- When you see $(x - 3)(x + 2)$, **FOIL** it to get $x^2 - x - 6$.

- When you see $\frac{12}{16}$, **reduce** it to $\frac{3}{4}$.

- When you see $\sqrt{50}$, **simplify** it to $5\sqrt{2}$ or just 7.07.

This is what the SAT wants you to do; these steps will usually bring you to the correct answer. I have seen this strategy dramatically help students, especially kids who get stuck and don't know what to do next—this strategy tells you what to do next.

Let's look at the question from the Pretest.

27. If $x^2 - y^2 = 36$ and $x - y = 12$, what is the value of $x + y$?

Solution: If you see $x^2 - y^2$, factor it.

$x^2 - y^2 = 36$
$(x - y)(x + y) = 36$ factor $x^2 - y^2$ to $(x - y)(x + y)$
$12(x + y) = 36$ substitute in 12 for $(x - y)$, since $(x - y) = 12$
$x + y = 3$ divide both sides by 12

Correct answer: 3

Just Do It! . . . Springboard Drills

Medium

1 If $\frac{3}{18} = \frac{a}{k}$ and a and k are integers, then k could equal which of the following?

- Ⓐ 1
- Ⓑ 3
- Ⓒ 4
- Ⓓ 6
- Ⓔ 9

2 If $m = p(p + 2)$, then $m - 3 =$

- Ⓐ $p^2 - 2p$
- Ⓑ $p^2 + 2$
- Ⓒ $p^2 - 2p - 3$
- Ⓓ $p^2 + 2p - 3$
- Ⓔ $p^2 + 2p$

$p^2 + 2p - 3$

3 If $x^2 - y^2 = 108$ and $x + y = 9$, what is the value of $x - y$?

Hard

4 If m and n are constants and $x^2 + mx + 5$ equals $(x + n)(x + 1)$, what is the value of m ?

- Ⓐ 5
- Ⓑ 6
- Ⓒ 7
- Ⓓ 8
- Ⓔ 9

5 If $12\sqrt{12} = p\sqrt{q}$ and p and q are positive integers, where $p > q$, what is the value of $\frac{p}{q}$?

- Ⓐ 1
- Ⓑ 4
- Ⓒ 8
- Ⓓ 16
- Ⓔ 144

6 If $xy = 11$, $x^2 = 5$, and $y^2 = 7$, then $(x - 3y)^2 =$

- Ⓐ 0
- Ⓑ 2
- Ⓒ 35
- Ⓓ 121
- Ⓔ 385

Beyond Your Dear Aunt Sally: The Laws of Exponents I

The SAT loves to test the laws of exponents. I know that you think that the SAT is incapable of love, that they are a sadistic organization. But I used to teach yoga to the employees who make the SAT, and I can tell you that they are very **nearly** normal people.

Anyway, the SAT loves exponents; they are on every test. Memorize these rules. Practice working with them in the drills, and check your answers. Then teach them to a friend.

$n^6 \times n^2 = n^8$ When multiplying like bases, add exponents.

$\dfrac{n^6}{n^2} = n^4$ When dividing like bases, subtract exponents.

$(n^6)^2 = n^{12}$ Power to a power, multiply exponents.

$n^0 = 1$ Any base to the 0 power equals 1.

SAT Math Mantra #28
Memorize the laws of exponents.

Let's look at the question from the Pretest.

28. If m, n, and p are positive integers and $3^m \cdot 3^n \cdot 3^p = 81$, then the greatest possible value for p is

   (A) 1   (B) 2   (C) 3   (D) 4   (E) 5

Solution: Great SAT strategy: If you want one thing to be as big as possible, make the other things as small as possible. To maximize p, make m and n as small as possible. Since they must be positive, $m = n = 1$. So $3^1 \cdot 3^1 \cdot 3^p = 81$. Then "Use the Answers" and your calculator to see which answer choice works.

Correct answer: B

Easy

❶ What is the product of x^2 and $2x^3$?

Ⓐ $2x^5$

Ⓑ $2x^6$

Ⓒ $3x^5$

Ⓓ $4x^6$

Ⓔ $x^2 + 2x^3$

❷ What is the product of $3m^4$ and $2b^4$?

Ⓐ $5mb^8$

Ⓑ $6mb^8$

Ⓒ $6(mb)^4$

Ⓓ $5(mb)^8$

Ⓔ $6(mb)^8$

Medium

❸ If a and b are positive integers and $2^a \cdot 2^b = 64$, then the greatest possible value for b is

Ⓐ 1

Ⓑ 2

Ⓒ 3

Ⓓ 4

Ⓔ 5

❹ If m, n, and p are different positive integers and $2^m \cdot 2^n \cdot 2^p = 128$, then the greatest possible value for p is ?

Ⓐ 1

Ⓑ 2

Ⓒ 3

Ⓓ 4

Ⓔ 5

❺ If $p^m \cdot p^6 = p^{12}$ and $(p^3)^n = p^{21}$, what is the value of $n - m$?

Ⓐ 1

Ⓑ 2

Ⓒ 5

Ⓓ 12

Ⓔ 16

Hard

❻ If $a^4 = b^8$, what is the value of b in terms of a ?

Ⓐ $a^{\frac{1}{2}}$

Ⓑ $2a$

Ⓒ a^2

Ⓓ $(2a)^2$

Ⓔ a^3

$n^{-2} = \dfrac{1}{n^2}$ A negative exponent means "take the reciprocal."

$2n^2 + n^2 = 3n^2$ When adding with like bases and like exponents, add coefficients. Remember that n^2 means $1\ n^2$.

$2n + n^2$ These do not combine. Terms combine only if they have like bases and like exponents.

$n^{4/3} = \sqrt[3]{n^4}$ For a fractional exponent, the top number is the power and the bottom number is the root.

Now, let's take a look at the question from the Pretest.

29. If $8m^2p^3 = m^5p$, what is m in terms of p ?

   (A) $p^{2/3}$ (B) $2p^{2/3}$ (C) $8p^{2/3}$ (D) $2p^2$ (E) $8p^{-2}$

Solution: Great review of Skill 2, "What is m in terms of p" means solve for m, use algebra to get m alone.

$8m^2p^3 = m^5p$	divide both sides by p
$8m^2p^2 = m^5$	divide both sides by m^2
$8p^2 = m^3$	put both sides to the one-third exponent, since $(m^3)^{1/3} = m$
$(8p^2)^{1/3} = m$	distribute the exponent
$2p^{2/3} = m$	

Correct answer: B

Far Beyond Your Dear Aunt Sally:
The Laws of Exponents II Drills

Medium

① What is the sum of $2x^2$ and $2x^3$?

Ⓐ $4x^5$

Ⓑ $2x^6$

Ⓒ $2x^2 + 2x^3$

Ⓓ $2x^4 + 2x^4$

Ⓔ $(2x^2)(2x^3)$

② What is the sum of $4x^2$ and $5x^2$?

Ⓐ $9x^4$

Ⓑ $9x^2$

Ⓒ $4x^2 + 5x^2$

Ⓓ $20x^4$

Ⓔ $20x^2$

③ The product of $3m^{-2}$ and $2m^{-5}$ is

Ⓐ $\dfrac{6}{m^7}$

Ⓑ $\dfrac{1}{6m^7}$

Ⓒ $5m^7$

Ⓓ $6m^7$

Ⓔ $\dfrac{5}{m^7}$

Hard

④ If n and p are positive integers and $3^{n/p} = \sqrt{27}$, then the product of n and p is

Ⓐ -1

Ⓑ 0

Ⓒ 3

Ⓓ 6

Ⓔ 9

⑤ If $p^m \cdot p^{-4} = p^5$ and $(p^{-2})^n = p^{20}$, what is the value of $n - m$?

Ⓐ -1

Ⓑ -2

Ⓒ -5

Ⓓ -12

Ⓔ -19

⑥ If m, n, and p are negative integers and $3^m \cdot 3^n \cdot 3^p = (243)^{-1}$, then nmp could equal

Ⓐ -1 or -2

Ⓑ -2 or -3

Ⓒ -3 or -4

Ⓓ -4 or -5

Ⓔ -5 or -6

In school, we usually use $y = mx + b$ for the equation of a line. For some reason, the SAT often uses $y = ax + b$ and this confuses students. Just know that it's the same. This is the kind of thing that can throw someone. But remember, by the time you are done with this workbook, you will know everything you need for the test; there are no surprises. Be confident. Don't be intimidated; know what you know. I'm not telling you to be arrogant, just self-assured. If you feel yourself getting thrown, relax your body, breathe deeply, chill, use your math mantras, and figure it out—you are a math ninja!

For the equation $y = mx + b$ or $y = ax + b$, m or a is the slope, sometimes called the rate of change, and b is the y intercept (the place where the line crosses the y axis). Often this knowledge is enough to get a question correct.

Note: If you are given a point (x, y) and the equation of a line, usually you need to plug the point into the equation and solve for a variable.

SAT Math Mantra #30
**For the equation $y = mx + b$ or $y = ax + b$, m or a is the slope
and b is the y intercept.**

Let's take a look at the question from the Pretest.

30. If McLovin's lawn-mowing service charges $25 to come to a house and $0.50 for each bag of leaves that they remove, which of the following equations express McLovin's fees for a visit if he removes x bags of leaves?

(A) $y = 25$
(B) $y = 25x + 0.5$
(C) $y = 0.5x$
(D) $y = 0.5x + 25$
(E) $y = 25x$

Solution: This is a great question to review because I see it in a lot of SATs lately. The fee for each bag, $0.50, is the amount that depends on the number of bags, so that goes next to the x, whereas $25 is a fixed fee, unrelated to how many bags McLovin hauls. So $y = 0.50x + 25$.

Correct answer: D

Your Algebra Teacher Never Said "$y = ax + b$" Drills

Note: The following questions are out of Easy, Medium, Hard order because of the length of #3 and available room on the page.

Easy

❶ If a movie offends 50 people in a theater just by the title of the movie, and 25 more people with each joke, which of the following equations express the number of people offended after x number of jokes?

Ⓐ $y = 50$
Ⓑ $y = 50x + 25$
Ⓒ $y = 25x$
Ⓓ $y = 75x$
Ⓔ $y = 25x + 50$

❷ If $(2, g)$ is a solution to the equation $y = -2x + 3$, then $g =$

Hard

❸ If the equation of line j is $y = mx - 2$ and line k is perpendicular to line j at the point $(2, 1)$, what is the equation of line k ?

Ⓐ $y = 2x + 3$
Ⓑ $y = \frac{4}{3}x - \frac{1}{3}$
Ⓒ $y = \frac{2}{3}x$
Ⓓ $y = -\frac{3}{2}x$
Ⓔ $y = -\frac{2}{3}x + \frac{7}{3}$

Medium

❹ For the equation $y = ax + b$, Alex knew that b should be 4 and that the slope was positive. Which of the following could be the graph of this line?

Ⓐ

Ⓑ

Ⓒ

Ⓓ

Ⓔ

Arrangements I

Arrangement questions ask you how many arrangements of something are possible, like how many different ways four letters can be arranged. Every test has at least one of these. Arrangement questions seem impossible to many students, but they are easy if you know the steps:

Step 1. Draw a blank for each position.
Step 2. Fill in the # of possibilities to fill each position.
Step 3. Multiply.

> Let's take this strategy for a spin on the question from the Pretest.
>
> 31. Fletch F. Fletch buys an ice cream sundae that contains one scoop of ice cream, one sauce, and either a cherry or pineapple wedge on top. He can choose chocolate, vanilla, strawberry, or banana ice cream; he can choose chocolate, caramel, or berry sauce; and he can choose either the cherry or the pineapple wedge for the top. How many different arrangements of these ingredients for Fletch's ice cream sundae are possible?

Solution:

❶ Draw a blank for each position.

$$\underline{\hspace{2cm}} \times \underline{\hspace{2cm}} \times \underline{\hspace{2cm}}$$

    ice cream   syrup   cherry or
    flavor   flavor   pineapple

❷ Enter the number of possibilities that can fill each position.

$$\underline{\quad 4 \quad} \times \underline{\quad 3 \quad} \times \underline{\quad 2 \quad}$$

    ice cream   syrup   cherry or
    flavor   flavor   pineapple

❸ Multiply the numbers to get the number of arrangements! $4 \times 3 \times 2 = 24$

Correct answer: 24

SAT Math Mantra #31
When you see an arrangement question, draw a blank for each position,
fill in the # of possibilities to fill each position, and multiply.

Arrangements I Drills

Easy

1 For a fund raiser, the meditation club is selling tee-shirts with a choice of two slogans, "See clearly" or "Non-attachment." Each shirt is available in small, medium, or large. How many different types of shirts are available?

2 Five actors are being cast to fill five roles. If each actor plays only one role, how many different arrangements of actors in the five roles are possible?

Ⓐ 5
Ⓑ 10
Ⓒ 60
Ⓓ 120
Ⓔ 240

3 At the build-your-own-burrito bar, you can choose chicken, beef, or shrimp. You can include no vegetable, spinach, or sautéed zucchini; and you can top it with mild, medium, hot, or killer salsa. How many different burritos can be ordered?

Ⓐ 8
Ⓑ 18
Ⓒ 24
Ⓓ 36
Ⓔ 48

Medium

4 The four digits 1, 2, 3, and 4 are used to form a number in which no digit is used more than once. How many such numbers are possible?

Ⓐ 8
Ⓑ 16
Ⓒ 18
Ⓓ 21
Ⓔ 24

5 How many different three-digit positive integers have only prime numbers as digits?

$$\phi \ \gamma \ \varphi \ \lambda \ \varpi$$

6 Kyle will write 3 different symbols shown above on a banner. How many such arrangements are possible?

Arrangements II

The arrangements in Skill 31 would be easy or medium questions. More "difficult" questions usually include a "restriction" or a "team." To solve these questions, we follow the same steps; but for a restriction we fill in the restricted positions first, and for a team we divide by 2.

Here's the question from the Pretest.

32. On a touch-football team there are 5 kids who will be assigned to fill the 5 positions: 1 quarterback, 3 receivers, and 1 lineman. If only 3 kids can play quarterback or lineman, how many arrangements of the team are possible?

Step 1. $\underline{\hspace{2cm}}$ $\underline{\hspace{1.5cm}}$ $\underline{\hspace{1.5cm}}$ $\underline{\hspace{1.5cm}}$ $\underline{\hspace{2cm}}$
     Quarterback   W.R.   W.R.   W.R.   Lineman

Step 2. Fill in restricted positions first.

       $\underline{\ \ 3\ \ }$ $\underline{\ \ 3\ \ }$ $\underline{\ \ 2\ \ }$ $\underline{\ \ 1\ \ }$ $\underline{\ \ 2\ \ }$
     Quarterback   W.R.   W.R.   W.R.   Lineman

Three players can play quarterback or lineman, so we fill in 3 for quarterback and 2 for lineman, since 1 of the 3 has now been assigned to quarterback. Then we fill in the rest of the blanks. Two players have been assigned to QB and lineman, so 3 remain to be assigned to the first wide receiver slot, then 2, then 1.

Step 3. Multiply the numbers.

Correct answer: 36

Teams

Team questions have duplicates that we should not double-count. Here's an example: There are 12 children in a class. Two will be chosen as a team to hide for a game. How many such teams of two children are possible?

Step 1. Draw a blank for each of the two children on the team.
Step 2. Fill in the number of possibilities for each blank.
Step 3. Multiply the numbers. $12 \times 11 = 132$. Normally you'd be done, but here we have one final step. We divide the answer by 2 since there are duplicates. For this team of two kids, it doesn't matter if it's Jimmy and Jill or Jill and Jimmy, so there are exactly twice as many answers as there should be. This rule works for any team of 2. (Once the SAT used a team of 3, and then we would divide by the number 6, but usually they use teams of 2 and we divide by the number 2.)

> **SAT Math Mantra #32**
> When an arrangement question mentions a "restriction,"
> fill in the restricted positions first.
> When an arrangement question mentions a "team of two,"
> divide your result by 2.

Arrangements II Drills

Medium

1 Of the six members of the girls' tennis club, two will compete as the doubles team. How many different such teams of two girls are possible?

2 The three digits 1, 2, and 3 are used form a number in which no digit is used more than once. How many such numbers greater than 200 are possible?

(A) 2
(B) 4
(C) 6
(D) 8
(E) 22

Hard

3 How many four-digit positive integers are even?

(A) 450
(B) 625
(C) 4500
(D) 5000
(E) 10,000

4 How many different three-digit positive integers have a prime units digit?

$$\phi \ \gamma \ \varphi \ \lambda \ \varpi$$

5 The 5 symbols above are written so that γ is never in the middle; it is always on one of the ends. How many such arrangements are possible?

6 There are 6 kids waiting to be chosen to fill the five positions in a stickball game. If, of the 6 kids, only 3 are skilled enough to pitch or catch, how many arrangements of the 6 kids in the five positions are possible?

(A) 72
(B) 120
(C) 144
(D) 720
(E) 1440

Tell Me What You Want, What You Really Really Want . . . Probability

They don't take the SAT over there in England, but Scary, Baby, Ginger, Posh, and Sporty summed up probability in 1996. Like functions, probability could be the topic of a college course, but the SAT asks only one thing! To find out about that one thing, please get out your credit card and see my website.

I'm kidding. The one thing is $\text{Probability} = \frac{\text{want}}{\text{total}}$

In English that's "Probability equals what you want, divided by the total number of things you are choosing from." Thanks again to Scary, Baby, and the gang.

Let's see that on the Pretest.

33. Of the 24 chocolates in a box, 10 are solid milk chocolates, 10 are solid dark chocolates, and 4 are cream-filled. If Noah randomly chooses a chocolate from the box, what is the probability that it will NOT be solid dark chocolate?

(A) $\frac{1}{12}$　　　(B) $\frac{1}{6}$　　　(C) $\frac{5}{12}$　　　(D) $\frac{7}{12}$　　　(E) $\frac{5}{6}$

Solution: Anytime you see "probability," use the equation $\text{Probability} = \frac{\text{want}}{\text{total}}$. We want anything but solid dark chocolate, so there are 14 we'd be happy with and that number goes on top. The total number of chocolates to choose from is 24, so that number goes on bottom. So the probability of not selecting a solid dark chocolate is $\frac{14}{24} = \frac{7}{12}$.

Correct answer: D

Probability in school could be much harder than that, but it's NEVER harder on the SAT. $\text{Probability} = \frac{\text{want}}{\text{total}}$ is all they ask!

SAT Math Mantra #33
When you see "probability," use the equation Probability = $\frac{\text{want}}{\text{total}}$.

Tell Me What You Want, What You Really Really Want . . . Probability Drills

Easy

1 If 4 out of 12 marbles in a bag are blue, what is the probability that a marble selected at random from the bag will be blue?

Ⓐ $\frac{5}{6}$

Ⓑ $\frac{1}{3}$

Ⓒ $\frac{2}{3}$

Ⓓ $\frac{3}{4}$

Ⓔ 1

Medium

$$\{1, 4, 5, 6, 7, 8\}$$

2 What is the probability of randomly choosing a prime number from the set above?

3 A vegetable is to be chosen at random from a basket of vegetables. The probability that the vegetable chosen is a carrot is $\frac{1}{4}$. Which of the following could be the number of vegetables in the basket?

Ⓐ 5

Ⓑ 6

Ⓒ 7

Ⓓ 8

Ⓔ 9

4 A certain movie has c scenes containing obscenities and n scenes free of obscenities. If a scene is picked at random from the movie and the probability of obscenities is $\frac{7}{12}$, what is the value of $\frac{n}{c}$?

Ⓐ $\frac{7}{5}$

Ⓑ $\frac{12}{7}$

Ⓒ $\frac{5}{7}$

Ⓓ $\frac{7}{12}$

Ⓔ $\frac{5}{6}$

Hard

5 In game 1 of the finals, Northampton will play Amherst. In game 2 Amherst will play Hadley. In game 3 Hadley will play Northampton. If, in each game, either team has an equal chance of winning, what is the probability that Northampton will win both its games?

He's Making a List . . . Median and Mode

Median and mode questions test one thing. They test whether you know the words "median" and "mode." Know the terms, and you will get these questions right every time.

Median is the middle number in a list of numbers.
Mode is the number that occurs the most often.

Consider this list: 5, 7, 9, 9, 11, 12, 12, 15, 15, 15, 15.
The median is 12 (it's in the middle of the list).
The mode is 15 (it occurs most often, 4 times).
That's it. It's that easy.

When you see a median or mode question:

* If the list of numbers is not in order, rewrite the numbers in order.
* If the numbers are given in a table, rewrite them as a list.
* Remember that increasing the value of any number above the median does not change the median.
* Also remember that decreasing the value of any number below the median does not change it.

Let's take a look at the question from the Pretest.

34. The median of a set of 9 consecutive integers is 42. What is the greatest of these 9 numbers?

Solution: Simply draw blanks for the 9 numbers and place 42 in the middle blank. Then fill in the consecutive numbers above and below 42. "Consecutive" means numbers in a row, for example, 42, 43, 44, 45, 46. So the greatest number is 46.

Correct answer: 46

SAT Math Mantra #34
When you see "median" or "mode," rewrite the data as a list in order.

He's Making a List . . . Median and Mode Drills

Medium

❶ The median of a set of 7 consecutive numbers is 31. What is the smallest of these 7 numbers?

Score	Number of Bowlers
150	2
145	3
140	1
135	2
130	4
125	2

❷ The scores on Wednesday's Bowling League for 14 bowlers are shown in the table above. Don finished late, and his score was not shown in the table. If he received a score of 140, what is the value of the median minus the mode?

Ⓐ 5
Ⓑ 10
Ⓒ 15
Ⓓ 20
Ⓔ 25

Hard

❸ If $2m - 2$, $m + 3$, and $3m - 4$ are all integers and $2m - 2$ is the mode of these integers, which of the following could be a value for m?

Ⓐ 2
Ⓑ 4
Ⓒ 6
Ⓓ 8
Ⓔ 10

❹ In a set of nine different numbers, which of the following CANNOT affect the value of the median?

Ⓐ Increase each number by 4.
Ⓑ Increase the smallest number only.
Ⓒ Decrease the largest number only.
Ⓓ Increase the largest number only.
Ⓔ Triple each number.

Week	Attendance
1	531
2	452
3	x
4	357
5	389

❺ The table above shows attendance at school football games for the past five weeks. If no two weeks had the same attendance and the median attendance for the five weeks was 452, what is the least possible value of x?

$$y = ax^2 + bx + c$$

The graph of the equation $y = ax^2 + bx + c$ forms a U shape called a parabola. The equation is called "quadratic," which is just fancy vocab for having an x^2 term. In this equation, the a tells whether the U-shaped graph opens up or down, and the c is the y-intercept, the place where the graph crosses the y axis. That's all you need to know.

$$y = -ax^2 + bx + c$$

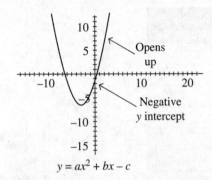

$$y = ax^2 + bx - c$$

Let's look at the question from the Pretest.

35. If the graph of $y = ax^2 + bx + c$ is shown above, then the value of ac can be

    I. Positive
   II. Negative
  III. 0

  (A) I only   (B) II only   (C) I or II   (D) I or III   (E) I, II, or III

Solution: Great question! From the diagram, we can tell that the U opens up, so the value of a must be positive, and the y intercept is negative, so c is negative. Thus, $(a)(c)$ must be negative, since a positive number times a negative number equals a negative number: $(+)(-) = (-)$.

Correct answer: B

SAT Math Mantra #35
For the equation $y = ax^2 + bx + c$, the a tells whether the U-shaped graph opens up or down, and the c is the y intercept.

Also, remember from Skill 30, when you are given a point (x, y) and an equation, plug the point into the equation.

$y = ax^2 + bx + c$ Drills

Medium

1 In the *xy* coordinate system, the graph of $y = 2x^2 + 3x + 4$ intersects $y = -x^2 + 3x + 4$ at $(0, k)$. What is the value of *k* ?

- Ⓐ 0
- Ⓑ 1
- Ⓒ 2
- Ⓓ 3
- Ⓔ 4

Hard

2 In the *xy* coordinate system, the graph of $y = 2x^2 + 3x + 4$ intersects $y = -x^2 + 3x + 4$ at $(m, 4)$. How many values for *m* satisfy the above equation?

- Ⓐ 0
- Ⓑ 1
- Ⓒ 2
- Ⓓ 3
- Ⓔ 4

3 In the *xy* coordinate system, the graph of $y = 2x^2 + 4$ intersects $y = -x^2 - k$ at $(m, 22)$. If *m* and *k* are integers, what is the value of *k* ?

- Ⓐ 31
- Ⓑ 3
- Ⓒ 0
- Ⓓ −3
- Ⓔ −31

4 Which of the following could be the graph of $y = kx^2 + 3x + r$, if *k* and *r* are negative constants?

Ⓐ

Ⓑ

Ⓒ

Ⓓ

Ⓔ

In the past few years, logic questions have been showing up more often. Of the several types of logic questions that you will see in the drills, there are two that give kids some trouble.

The first type gives a statement and asks you to make a conclusion. For example, "If Brian Leaf is very cool, then which of the following can you conclude?" And the correct answer might be something like, "If you meet Brian Leaf, he will be cool." The key to these questions is: do not get intimidated. Sometimes the answer, even to a "medium" question is so silly-obvious that you think, "I must be wrong, it can't be this ridiculous," but it is. So don't say, "I have no shot at this question." Say, "OK, I have been expecting you and you are mine." They are always easy if you chill.

The second type is "Spanish Club and Ski Team questions." Here's an example: There are 10 members of the Spanish Club and 10 members of the Ski Team, but 3 people belong to both. If the Spanish Club and Ski Team hold a joint meeting, how many people will attend? To determine the total members who will attend, just subtract: 20 − 3 = 17 since 3 people have been counted twice. So 17 people will be at the meeting.

Let's review the Pretest question.

36. At New Leaf High School some students who do yoga also run cross-country, and no one who runs cross-country is on the fencing team. Which of the following must also be true of the students at New Leaf High School?

(A) No one fences.
(B) No one who does yoga is a fencer.
(C) More students run cross-country than do yoga.
(D) More students do yoga than fence.
(E) Some of the students who do yoga do not fence.

Solution: If some students who do yoga also run cross-country and no one who runs cross-country fences, then some of the yoga students must not fence. The only way to get this one wrong is to rush into one of the first four wrong choices or to doubt yourself and say, "I don't get this, I'll just go with B." But if you stay relaxed and focused and confident, you can see that choice E is the correct answer.

Correct answer: E

SAT Math Mantra #36
Logic questions are easy long as you stay focused and do NOT get intimidated.

"That's Illogical, Captain" Drills

Medium

1 Brian Leaf, principal of New Leaf High School, wears sandals to work everyday that it is sunny, cloudy, or snowing, but not days that it is raining. If today Brian is wearing sandals, we can conclude that

  Ⓐ It is sunny.
  Ⓑ It is sunny or cloudy.
  Ⓒ It is not snowing.
  Ⓓ It is not raining.
  Ⓔ Tomorrow it will rain.

2 The sums of the weights of groups of three animals are measured and ordered from least to greatest as follows:

The weight of the pig, sheep, and goat
The weight of the pig, sheep, and mule
The weight of the pig, goat, and mule
The weight of the sheep, goat, and mule

Which of the following arrangements expresses the weights of the four animals from least to greatest?

  Ⓐ Goat < pig < sheep < mule
  Ⓑ Mule < goat < sheep < pig
  Ⓒ Mule < sheep < goat < pig
  Ⓓ Goat < mule < pig < sheep
  Ⓔ Pig < sheep < goat < mule

Use the following diagram for Questions 3 and 4.

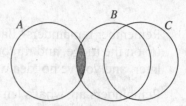

3 In the figure above, region A represents the set of all even numbers, region B represents the set of all prime numbers, and region C represents the set of odd numbers less than 50. Which of the following numbers could be a member of the set represented by the shaded region?

  Ⓐ 0
  Ⓑ 1
  Ⓒ 2
  Ⓓ 3
  Ⓔ 4

4 How many members does the intersection of region B and region C contain?

  Ⓐ 14
  Ⓑ 15
  Ⓒ 24
  Ⓓ 25
  Ⓔ More than 25

5 The Environmental Club and the Spanish Club both have 23 members, and at a fully attended joint meeting of the two clubs, there were 40 members. How many individuals belong to both clubs?

Remember remainders? Back in 5th grade you had this thing down. You learned it, put it up on the fridge, and ran out into the yard for prisoner dodgeball. But now it's six years later, and you've no idea what I'm talking about.

Remainders are what's left over when you use long division.

$$\begin{array}{r} 52\ r1 \\ 7\overline{)365} \\ -35 \\ \hline 15 \\ -14 \\ \hline 1 \end{array}$$

For example:

The r1 means remainder 1. That's it. So why is this on the SAT? I think that years ago, when the SAT made the decision to allow calculators on the test, they started using remainder questions since they are hard to do with a calculator. But the Buddha said that if a man is shot by an arrow, do not waste time on discovering who shot him, just help him. So here's the help. Remainders are easy, and as usual, the SAT always asks the same concepts.

Let's take a look at the Pretest question.

37. All the following numbers have remainder 3 when divided by 4 EXCEPT

(A) 7   (B) 15   (C) 22   (D) 23   (E) 31

Solution: This is a great review of our "Use the Answers" strategy. Just try each number to see which answer choice does not give remainder 3, when divided by 4.

$$\begin{array}{r} 1\ r3 \\ 4\overline{)7} \\ 4 \\ \hline 3 \end{array} \qquad \begin{array}{r} 3\ r3 \\ 4\overline{)15} \\ 12 \\ \hline 3 \end{array} \qquad \begin{array}{r} 5\ r2 \\ 4\overline{)22} \\ 20 \\ \hline 2 \end{array} \qquad \begin{array}{r} 5\ r3 \\ 4\overline{)23} \\ 20 \\ \hline 3 \end{array} \qquad \begin{array}{r} 7\ r3 \\ 4\overline{)31} \\ 28 \\ \hline 3 \end{array}$$

Each choice works EXCEPT choice C, 22, which gives a remainder of 2 not 3.

Correct answer: C

SAT Math Mantra #37
Remainders are what's left over when you use long division.

Hopscotch, Pigtails, and Remainders Drills

Medium

1 What is the remainder when 13 is divided by 3 ?

- Ⓐ 0
- Ⓑ 1
- Ⓒ 2
- Ⓓ 3
- Ⓔ 4

2 All the following can be the remainders of 24 divided by an even number EXCEPT

- Ⓐ 12
- Ⓑ 10
- Ⓒ 8
- Ⓓ 6
- Ⓔ 4

3 All the following numbers have the same remainder when divided by 4 EXCEPT

- Ⓐ 7
- Ⓑ 15
- Ⓒ 19
- Ⓓ 22
- Ⓔ 27

Hard

4 Which of the following could be remainders when five consecutive positive integers are each divided by 4 ?

- Ⓐ 1, 2, 3, 0, 1
- Ⓑ 1, 2, 3, 4, 1
- Ⓒ 1, 2, 0, 1, 2
- Ⓓ 0, 1, 2, 1, 0
- Ⓔ 0, 4, 3, 2, 1

5 For all negative integers m and n, let $m \, \Re \, n$ be defined as the remainder when n is divided by m. If $-18 \, \Re \, n = 3$, which of the following can be the value of n ?

- Ⓐ -18
- Ⓑ -36
- Ⓒ -41
- Ⓓ 36
- Ⓔ 39

6 For all integers p and q, let $p \Theta q$ be defined as the remainder when p is divided by q. How many different values for b make the statement $24 \Theta b = 3$ true?

- Ⓐ 0
- Ⓑ 1
- Ⓒ 2
- Ⓓ 3
- Ⓔ 4

Absolute Value

The expression $|-3|$ means "the absolute value of -3." The $|\ |$ bars mean absolute value. Like many SAT topics, this is really just vocab. If you don't know the meaning of the term, then it's very hard or impossible to get the question correct; but if you know the vocab, it's EASY!

Basically, absolute value just means, "Ditch the negative sign!" $|-3| = 3$ and $|3| = 3$. So it does not mean to switch the sign necessarily; it just means drop the $(-)$ negative signs, which makes it positive. You do this only after you've done what is between the bars. For example, $|-3 - 6| = |-9| = 9$. You don't just drop negative signs right away. First you do the math between the bars, and when you've done all the math that you can, then you drop the negative sign.

Here's the key to absolute value on the SAT: usually you have to come up with the less obvious answer to the question. For example, of course 3 is one answer to $|x - 1| = 2$, but -1 is also an answer, and that's the one you'll need on the SAT. How do you find the less obvious answer? Drop the bars and switch the sign of the answer: $x - 1 = -2$; then solve for x.

That's it. That's absolute value. If you did not know this and you do by the end of the drills, then you will gain points!

Let's practice.

38. Which of the following are solutions to $|n + 3| = 5$?

    I. 2   II. −2   III. −8

    (A) I only
    (B) III only
    (C) II and III
    (D) I and III
    (E) I, II, and III

Solution: Great "Use the Answers" review. Try each answer choice in the absolute value equation in the question:

I. $|2 + 3| = 5$ correct   II. $|-2 + 3| \neq 5$ incorrect   III. $|-8 + 3| = 5$ correct
So I and III are correct and choice D is the answer.

Correct answer: D

SAT Math Mantra #38
When you see absolute value, look for the less obvious answer.

Absolute Value Drills

Easy

1 If $|6 - m| = 12$, then $m =$

Ⓐ 6 or 0

Ⓑ 12 or −6

Ⓒ 18 or −6

Ⓓ 18 or 6

Ⓔ 0 or −6

2 Which of the following are solutions to
$|p - 6| = 5$?

I. 11

II. 5

III. 1

Ⓐ I only

Ⓑ III only

Ⓒ II and III

Ⓓ I and III

Ⓔ I, II, and III

Medium

3 For negative integers m and n, if $|m| + |n| = 8$,
what is the least possible value for $m - n$?

Ⓐ 8

Ⓑ 0

Ⓒ −4

Ⓓ −6

Ⓔ −16

$$|4 + x| = 8$$
$$|3 - y| = 5$$

4 If in the equations above $x < 0$ and $y < 0$, what
is the value of xy ?

Ⓐ −32

Ⓑ −24

Ⓒ 6

Ⓓ 12

Ⓔ 24

5 If $|1 + 2a| < 1$, what is one possible value of a ?

Hard

6 If $m = |n|$, then m could equal

I. 0

II. n

III. $-n$

Ⓐ I only

Ⓑ III only

Ⓒ I and II

Ⓓ II and III

Ⓔ I, II, and III

Sequences I

There is a complex formula for sequence questions that you may or may not have used in school, but on the SAT we do not need it. There are only two kinds of sequence questions on the SAT (Skills 39 and 40). The first requires you to write out a bunch of terms and do something with them, such as find the sum or average.

Here's the question from the Pretest.

39. If a sequence begins with the number 3, and each term that follows is found by adding 4, what is the sum of the first 5 terms?

Solution: Write out the first 5 terms of the sequence, following the directions: 3, 7, 11, 15, 19. Then find the sum by adding these five terms.

Correct answer: 55

| SAT Math Matra #39 |
| To solve a sequence question, write out a bunch of terms. |

That was so easy to explain that I have some room left. So, here's Brian's Math Magic Trick #2.

Brian's Math Magic Trick #2
Choose a number between 1 and 10.
Multiply your number by 9.
Take the result and add the digits; for example, if your result was 26, then 2 + 6 = 8.
Now take that number and subtract 5.
Then correspond that number to the alphabet: 1 is A, 2 is B, 3 is C, 4 is D, 5 is E, and so on.
Choose a country that begins with that letter. Spell the country; what is the second letter?
And choose an animal that begins that letter. Now turn to the solutions for Skill 39.

Sequences I Drills

Easy

3, 6, 12, 24, . . .

1 In the sequence above, the first term is 3 and every number after that is found by doubling the preceding number. What is the 7th term in the sequence?

(A) 48

(B) 96

(C) 192

(D) 240

(E) 384

112, 54, 18, . . .

2 In the sequence above, each number after the first is $\frac{1}{3}$ of the preceding term. What is the 6th term of the sequence?

3 What is the greatest of four consecutive prime integers, if the least is integer is 11 ?

Medium

4 The first term in a sequence is 12, and the second term is 8. The third term and each term after the third are the average of the preceding two terms. What is the value of the first term in the sequence that is an odd number?

5 In a given sequence, the first term is 1, and every number after the first is found by adding 3 and then doubling the result. What is average of the first six terms in the sequence?

(A) 10.5

(B) 15.75

(C) 39

(D) 67.5

(E) 405

6 Sora started a ball at the 15-centimeter mark on a long tape measure. She then rolled it forward 6 centimeters. Before it stopped rolling, the ball would settle back toward her one unit. She continued this pattern until the ball reached the 60-centimeter mark. How many times did Sora roll the ball?

(A) 10

(B) 9

(C) 8

(D) 7

(E) 6

Sequences II

The second type of sequence question has a repeating pattern, like 1, 2, 3, 1, 2, 3. . . . To solve this type, write out terms until you see the repeating pattern. Then use the pattern to answer the question.

Let's take a look at the question from the Pretest.

40. A sequence begins with the number 5. The next term is found by adding 4, and the next is found by multiplying by −1. If this pattern of adding 4 and then multiplying by −1 is followed, what is the 26th term in the sequence?

   (A) −9　　　(B) −5　　　(C) 5　　　(D) 9　　　(E) 26

Solution: Follow the instructions for the sequence that are given in the question, until you notice a repeating pattern. Then use this repeating pattern to answer the question.

$$5, 9, -9, -5, 5, 9, -9, -5, 5$$

Bingo, there's the pattern. 5, 9, −9, −5, . . .
So use this pattern to count to the 26th term, which will be 9.

Correct answer: D

Sometimes the pattern does not repeat, but we can determine the amount that it changes between each term and use that to predict a later term. For example, in the pattern 3, 7, 11, 15, 19, . . . , each term after the first increases by 4. So if we wanted to predict the 105th term, we would add the first term, which is 3, to (104)(4), since there are 104 fours being added to reach the 105th term. 3 + (104)(4) = 419.

SAT Math Mantra #40
To solve a sequence question, write the next bunch of terms until you have as many as you need or until you see a repeating pattern.

These questions are easy once you are familiar with the language. Let's practice.

Sequences II Drills

Medium

3, 6, 9, 12, . . .

① In the sequence above, the first term is 3 and every number after that is found by adding 3 to the preceding number. What is the 77th term in the sequence?

- Ⓐ 231
- Ⓑ 232
- Ⓒ 233
- Ⓓ 234
- Ⓔ 235

② Jenny started a ball at the 15-centimeter mark on a long tape measure. She then rolled it forward 6 centimeters. Before it stopped rolling, the ball settled back toward her one unit. If Jenny continued this pattern for a *total* of 41 rolls, what mark would the ball reach?

- Ⓐ 220
- Ⓑ 230
- Ⓒ 250
- Ⓓ 261
- Ⓔ 289

③ Jason is writing the letters of his name around the margin of his paper. After he writes the 201st letter, what will be the next letter that he writes?

- Ⓐ J
- Ⓑ A
- Ⓒ S
- Ⓓ O
- Ⓔ N

Hard

3, 6, −6, . . .

④ The first term in the sequence of numbers shown above is 3. The sequence above continues by adding 3 to every odd-numbered term and multiplying every even-numbered term by −1. For example, the second term is $3 + 3$, and the third term is $(-1) \times 6$. What is the 41st term in the sequence?

⑤ A sequence of terms begins with $2x$. Each additional term is found by doubling the preceding term. What is the value of the nth term?

- Ⓐ $2x$
- Ⓑ $2nx$
- Ⓒ $2x^n$
- Ⓓ x^2n
- Ⓔ $2^n x$

3, 0, . . .

⑥ The sequence above continues by subtracting 3 from every odd-numbered term and multiplying every even-numbered term by −1. For example, the second term is $3 - 3$, and the third term is $(-1) \times 0$. What is the 167th term in the sequence?

- Ⓐ −3
- Ⓑ −1
- Ⓒ 0
- Ⓓ 3
- Ⓔ 6

Don't Even Think about It! . . . Most Common SAT Math Careless Errors I

On average, after memorizing and practicing Skills 41 and 42 for avoiding careless errors, most students gain 20 to 30 points! So learn these strategies.

Most Common SAT Math Careless Errors

1 Practice being focused, yet relaxed. You don't need to be tense and a wreck to excel on the SAT or in life. You can be intense and work quickly, yet be relaxed. Be fully present with each question: focused, relaxed, awake, and mindful. See "A Yoga Posture for the SAT," page 60.

2 $(2x)^2 = 4x^2$, not $2x^2$. Square both the 2 and the x.

3 $-2(3x - 3) = -6x + 6$, not $-6x - 6$.

Remember to distribute the -2 to both the $3x$ and the -3.

4 $\frac{5x + 20}{5} = x + 4$, not $x + 20$

Remember that the 5 is under not only the $5x$, but also the 20.

Let's look at the Pretest question.

41. If $f(x) = 3x^2$, which of the following expresses $f(2p)$?

    (A) $6p$
    (B) $6p^2$
    (C) $12p$
    (D) $12p^2$
    (E) $24p^3$

Solution: Nice functions review! This is SAT function question type I. The $f(2p)$ just means plug $2p$ in for x. So $f(2p) = 3(2p)^2 = 3(4p^2) = 12p^2$. Careless error buster: Remember that the 2 gets squared. Also remember order of operations: multiply 3 by 4 after squaring 2.

Correct answer: D

Don't Even Think about It! . . . Most Common SAT Math Careless Errors I Drills

Medium

1 If $f(x) = -2x^3$, which of the following expresses $f(-p)$?

(A) $-2p$

(B) $2p^3$

(C) $-2p^3$

(D) $8p^3$

(E) $-8p^3$

2 When $m = -1$, which of the following is equivalent to $m(2x^2 - 2)$?

(A) $-2x^2 + 2$

(B) $-2x^2 - 2$

(C) $2x^2 - 2$

(D) $2x^2 + 2$

(E) $x^2 + 2$

3 If, $y = \dfrac{3a - 15}{x}$ find y when $x = 3$.

(A) $a - 15$

(B) $9a - 15$

(C) $9a - 5$

(D) $a - 5$

(E) $a - 3$

Hard

4 If $m = 2p$, then which of the following is equivalent to $(m + 4)^2$?

(A) $2p + 4$

(B) $4p^2 + 4$

(C) $2p^2 + 8p + 16$

(D) $4p^2 + 8p + 16$

(E) $4p^2 + 16p + 16$

5 If $f(x) = x(2x^2 - 2)$, find $f(-2p)$.

(A) $-16p^3 + 4p$

(B) $-8p^3 + 4p$

(C) $-8p^3 - 4p$

(D) $16p^3 - 4p$

(E) $8p^3 + 4p$

$$f(x) = x(x - 2)$$
$$g(x) = 3x$$

6 For functions f and g above, if $g(m) = 27$, find $f(-2m)$.

Don't Even Think about It! . . . Most Common SAT Math Careless Errors II

"Careless errors are bad mmmkay." So let's learn to avoid three more of the most common ones.

⑤ $(x + 3)^2 = (x + 3)(x + 3) = x^2 + 6x + 9$, not $x^2 + 9$
Remember the middle term when you FOIL.

⑥ $2(3)^2 = 18$, not 36
Remember your old friend PEMDAS, order of operation:
Parenthesis, Exponents, Multiplication/Division, Addition/Subtraction

⑦ Remember to finish the question. Sometimes you have solved for x, but the question asks for y or $3x - 2$. So before you grid each answer, take a moment to pause and say, "Wait (insert your name here), did I finish the question?" This is so simple, but hugely important. This is the most common careless error, and it's so easy to avoid!

SAT Math Mantra #42
"Careless errors are bad mmmkay," so underline all vocabulary words
and remember to finish the question.

Many students lose tons of points to careless errors. Don't do that. Memorize the above rules and practice watching for them. Be focused, relaxed, and mindful, and you will not make careless errors. You will be a math ninja, and like most ninja of ancient Japan, you will ace the SAT.

Pretest question:

42. For the equation $y = -3x^3 - 2$, when $x = 1$, what is the value of $-2y$?

Solution: When $x = 1$, $y = -3(1)^2 - 2 = -5$. Careless error buster: Remember to finish the question. The question does not ask for y, but for $-2y$. So the correct answer is $-2(-5) = 10$. This is weird since your math teacher always asks for y not $-2y$, but we know to watch for it and we avoid the careless error.

Correct answer: 10

Don't Even Think about It! . . . Most Common SAT Math Careless Errors II Drills

Medium

1 If $f(x) = 3x^2$, which of the following expresses $f(4p)$?

Ⓐ $12p^2$

Ⓑ $32p^2$

Ⓒ $48p^2$

Ⓓ $64p^2$

Ⓔ $144p^2$

$$y = 2x^2 + 4$$

2 When $x = -2$ in the equation above, what is the value of $y + 2$?

3 John rode his bicycle 5 miles to school in 10 minutes, and at the same speed, he later rode his bicycle to a friend's house 4 miles away. How many minutes would it take him to ride there?

Ⓐ 0.5

Ⓑ 1

Ⓒ 2

Ⓓ 4

Ⓔ 8

Hard

4 If $x = 3y$, then which of the following is equivalent to $(x - 2)^2$?

Ⓐ $3y - 2$

Ⓑ $3y^2 - 4$

Ⓒ $3y^2 + 6y - 4$

Ⓓ $9y^2 - 12y + 4$

Ⓔ $9y^2 + 18y + 4$

$$p(x) = 2x(x - 2)$$
$$r(x) = \frac{x}{3}$$

5 For functions p and r above, if $r(-6) = n$, find $p(-2n)$.

6 Josh rode his bicycle from his house to his grandmother's house at a rate of 10 miles per hour. Later that day he rode home at a rate of 15 miles per hour. If the round trip took a total of 30 minutes, how far does Josh live from his grandmother?

Misbehaving Numbers: Weird Number Behavior

The SAT tests your understanding of how certain weird numbers behave, such as when you subtract a negative, it's like adding, -6 is smaller than -1, and one-half squared gets smaller. You can know these, because here's the thing—the SAT always tests the same weird math behaviors. Here they are

① Small fractions multiplied by small fractions get smaller.
Usually when you multiply numbers, the result is larger than the originals, but small fractions get smaller.
Example: $\left(\frac{1}{2}\right)^2 = \frac{1}{2} \times \frac{1}{2} = \frac{1}{4}$

② The larger the digits of a negative number, the smaller it actually is.
Example: $-6 < -1$

③ Subtracting a negative number is like adding.
Example: $10 - (-4) = 14$

④ Squaring a negative eliminates it, but cubing does not.
Example: $(-3)^2 = 9$, but $(-3)^3 = -27$

⑤ Anything times zero equals zero.
Example: $(-16)(3)(0) = 0$

That's it. Know these and you will gain points, impress friends, and in general be a more attractive person.

Let's see if you're ready to take this skill out for a spin. Here's the question from the Pretest.

43. If $0.5mno = 0$ and $4nop = 12$, then which of the following must be true?

(A) $nop = 12$　　(B) $mno = -0.5$　　(C) $p = 0$　　(D) $m = 0$　　(E) $no = 3$

Solution: This is a great question. The SAT loves to see if you pick up on the zero stuff. In order to multiply to get zero, one of the numbers must be zero. And anything times zero equals zero. So $mno = 0$ and $nop \neq 0$, and therefore, m must equal zero.

Correct answer: D

Misbehaving Numbers: Weird Number Behavior Drills

Easy

1 If $q = 2kp$ and $k = 0$, what is the value of q ?

Medium

$\overset{\bullet}{N} \quad \overset{\bullet}{-4}$

2 On the number line above, which of the following could be represented by point N ?

Ⓐ 8

Ⓑ 4

Ⓒ 0

Ⓓ −3

Ⓔ −8

3 If $(x - 2)(x + 3) = 0$, then x could equal

   I. −3

   II. 0

   III. 2

Ⓐ II only

Ⓑ I and II

Ⓒ I and III

Ⓓ II and III

Ⓔ I, II, and III

4 If $m = -2$ and $n > 0$, which of the following is greatest?

Ⓐ mn

Ⓑ m^2n

Ⓒ m^3n

Ⓓ m^4n

Ⓔ m^5n

5 If $f(x) = 2f(x)$, then $f(x) =$

Ⓐ −1

Ⓑ 0

Ⓒ 1

Ⓓ 2

Ⓔ It cannot be determined from the information given.

6 If $r < 0$, which of the following is greatest?

Ⓐ r

Ⓑ $2 + r$

Ⓒ $2 - r$

Ⓓ $2 - r^2$

Ⓔ $2 + r^3$

Hard

7 If $-2 < x < -1$, then which of the following orders x, x^2, and x^3 from least to greatest?

Ⓐ $x < x^2 < x^3$

Ⓑ $x^2 < x^3 < x$

Ⓒ $x^3 < x < x^2$

Ⓓ $x < x^3 < x^2$

Ⓔ $x^3 < x^2 < x$

Mathematical Transformations

Transformations (and functions) are the only topics from Algebra II on the SAT. Transformations begin with a "parent" equation or graph, for example, $y = x^2$. It's called the parent because the transformed graphs are birthed/derived from it. A transformation happens when we add, subtract, multiply, or divide a number into the original that causes it to move it up, down, left, or right. It might even make it skinnier or fatter.

Here are all the transformations that the SAT uses:

$y = x^2 + 1$ moves every point of the graph up 1 unit.
$y = x^2 - 1$ moves every point of the graph down 1 unit.

$y = (x + 1)^2$ moves every point of the graph left 1 unit.

$y = (x - 1)^2$ moves every point of the graph right 1 unit.

$y = 2(x)^2$ makes the graph skinnier.

$y = 0.5(x)^2$ makes the graph fatter.

$y = -(x)^2$ reflects the graph across the x axis.

Let's practice using these:

44. The graph of $y = g(x)$ is shown below. Which of the following equations represents all the points of $g(x)$ shifted 1 unit to the left?

(A) $y = g(x) + 1$
(B) $y = g(x + 1)$
(C) $y = g(x - 1)$
(D) $y = g(x) - 1$
(E) $y = g(x)$

Solution: This is a straightforward transformation. The parent function $g(x)$ needs to be shifted 1 unit to the left. If you memorized the transformations shown above, this question is easy; a left transformation would be $y = g(x + 1)$. If you did not memorize the transformations, well . . . get to it, you silly slacker. Of course, you could also graph each choice on your calculator and see which one yields results that are all 1 unit to the left of the parent.

Correct answer: B

Mathematical Transformations Drills

Easy

① Which of the following could be the equation of the graph above?

Ⓐ $y = x - 1$
Ⓑ $y = x^2 - 1$
Ⓒ $y = (x - 1)^2$
Ⓓ $y = (x + 1)^2$
Ⓔ $y = x^2$

Medium

② The graph of $g(x)$ is shown above. Which of the following equations represents all the points of $g(x)$ shifted 1 unit to the right?

Ⓐ $y = g(x) + 1$
Ⓑ $y = g(x + 1)$
Ⓒ $y = g(x - 1)$
Ⓓ $y = g(x) + 1$
Ⓔ $y = g(x)$

Hard

③ Which of the following could represent all the points of the above graph moved 2 units down?

Ⓐ $y = x - 2$
Ⓑ $y = x^2 - 2$
Ⓒ $y = (x - 1)^2 - 2$
Ⓓ $y = (x + 1)^2 - 2$
Ⓔ $y = (x - 2)^2$

④ The figure above shows the graphs of the functions m and n. The function m is defined by $m(x) = x^3 + 2x$, and the function n is defined by $n(x) = m(x + h) - k$, where h and k are constants. What is the value of $h - k$?

Ⓐ 0
Ⓑ 1
Ⓒ 2
Ⓓ 3
Ⓔ 4

Weird Symbol Questions

The SAT invents symbols, like ♦, ⇑, ⊗, or ∀, to see if you can roll with it. Many students get thrown by these; they see a symbol that they don't recognize and think, "Shooters, I musta missed this in class while I was drawing scenes from *Twilight* on my binder." But remember, we know exactly what's on the test, and if you don't recognize something, then it must be a "Weird Symbol Question" and no one has seen it before. So instead of flippin' out, say, "Cool, a Weird Symbol Question, I LOVE these!" But perhaps not out loud during the test. The key to a weird symbol question is: just follow the directions given in the question. Weird symbol questions are always "mediums" or "hards" only because so many kids get weirded out by them. But they are easy!

Look at the question from the Pretest.

45. Let the operation ζ be defined by $m \zeta n = mn + m$. What is the value of $-2 \zeta 5$?

   (A) −12
   (B) −5
   (C) 0
   (D) 10
   (E) 14

Solution: Just follow the rule defined in the question: $m \zeta n = mn + m$. In other words, plug whatever numbers are given into $mn + m$ in place of the letters m and n:

$m \zeta n = mn + m$
$-2 \zeta 5 = (-2)(5) + (-2)$
$\qquad = -10 + (-2)$
$\qquad = -12$

So choice A is the answer. Easy.

Correct answer: A

SAT Math Mantra #45
When you see a weird symbol question: (1) relax, (2) remember that
no one has seen this symbol before, and (3) follow the directions given
in the question.

Weird Symbol Questions Drills

Medium

1 If m, n, and p are integers, let $m \wedge n \wedge p$ be defined to be true only if $p > m > n$. For $-3 \wedge n \wedge -1$, n can equal which of the following?

(A) 0

(B) −1

(C) −2

(D) −3

(E) −4

2 If r is a positive integer, let ⓡ be defined as the set of all prime factors of r. All the numbers in which of the following sets are also in all three of the sets ⑫ , ⑱ , ㉔ ?

(A) ⑤

(B) ⑭

(C) ㉕

(D) ㊱

(E) ㊳

3 Let the operation ⌐ be defined by $j \lrcorner l = (j + l)(j - l)$ for all numbers j and l. What is the value of $5 \lrcorner 4$?

Hard

4 Let $\lozenge x$ be defined as $\lozenge x = x^2 + 3x$ for all values of x. If $\lozenge m = \lozenge(m - 3)$, what is the value of m ?

(A) 0

(B) 1

(C) 2

(D) 3

(E) 4

5 Let the operation # be defined by $a \mathbin{\#} b = (a + 1)(b - 1)$ for all numbers a and b. If $m \mathbin{\#} 2 = 5 \mathbin{\#} 4$, what is the value of m ?

(A) 11

(B) 13

(C) 15

(D) 17

(E) 19

Directly Proportional

This is something that you learned for maybe two classes, three years ago in Algebra I. But, for some reason, it's on the SAT. Weird, but here's the good news: it's super easy. In fact, it's an "easy" topic for us because as long as you know what's on this page, it's cake; the reason it's rated "medium" or "hard" is because most students don't know it.

"Directly proportional" means "x times some number gives you y."
This table shows a "directly proportional" relationship because 4 multiplied by each x yields each y value.

x	y
2	8
3	12
4	16
5	20
6	24

The equation for the relationship in the table is $y = 4x$, and the equation for directly proportional in general is $y = kx$. Also since they are directly proportional, we can set up a proportion between any two (x, y) values in the table. For example: $\frac{2}{8} = \frac{3}{12}$.

Sometimes the SAT also calls this "varies directly," as in "y varies directly with x." This is exactly the same as "directly proportional."

That's it, that's all the SAT does with directly proportional.

Here's the question from the Pretest.

46. If y is directly proportional to x^3, and $y = 64$ when $x = 2$, what is x when $y = 216$?

Solution: "y is directly proportional to x^3" means $\frac{y}{x^3}$. So we set up a proportion between the two sets of (x, y) values and solve for the unknown x.

$$\frac{y}{x^3} = \frac{y}{x^3} \Rightarrow \frac{64}{2^3} = \frac{216}{x^3} \qquad \text{when you see a proportion, cross-multiply}$$

$64x^3 = (8)(216)$ simplify (8)(216)
$64x^3 = 1728$ divide both sides by 64
$\quad x^3 = 27$ take cube root of both sides
$\quad\; x = 3$

Correct answer: 3

Directly Proportional Drills

Medium

1 Which of the following expresses a relationship where y is directly proportional to x ?

(A)

x	y
1	1
2	4
3	9
4	16

(B)

x	y
1	5
2	10
3	15
4	20

(C)

x	y
1	2
2	3
3	4
4	5

(D)

x	y
1	2
2	6
3	12
4	16

(E)

x	y
1	1
2	3
3	5
4	7

2 If y is directly proportional to x^2, and $y = 18$ when $x = 3$, what is x when $y = 50$?

x	y
1	5
2	10
3	15
4	20

3 If y varies directly with x in the table above, what is the value of y when $x = 7.5$?

(A) 30
(B) 32.5
(C) 35
(D) 37.5
(E) 40

Hard

x	y
2	1
4	0.5
8	0.25
10	0.2

4 If y varies directly with x^{-1} in the table above, what is the value of y when $x = 5$?

(A) 0.5
(B) 0.4
(C) 0.3
(D) 0.2
(E) 0.1

Inversely Proportional

"Inversely proportional" means some number divided by x equals y.
This table shows an inverse proportion:

x	y
2	6
3	4
4	3
5	2.4
6	2

The equation for the relationship in the table is $y = \frac{12}{x}$, and the equation for inversely proportional, in general, is $y = \frac{k}{x}$. This also means that $xy = k$. In the SAT this is also called "inverse variation" or "varies inversely," as in "y varies inversely with x." Either way, it's the same.

Pretest question:

47. If y is inversely proportional to x and $y = 12$ when $x = 4$, what is the value of x when $y = 8$?

(A) 48
(B) 32
(C) 24
(D) 6
(E) 3

Solution: "y is inversely proportional to x" means $y = \frac{k}{x}$. Plug the first pair of values into this equation to find the value of k: $12 = \frac{k}{4}$. So $k = 48$. Now, using $k = 48$, plug the second pair of values $(x, 8)$ into the equation: $8 = \frac{48}{x}$. Cross-multiply $8x = 48$, so $x = 6$.

You could also use $xy = k$, so $(12)(4) = 48$, and $(x)(8)$ must also equal 48, so $x = 6$.

Correct answer: D

Inversely Proportional Drills

Medium

1 Which of the following expresses a relationship where y is inversely proportional to x ?

(A)

x	y
1	1
2	4
3	9
4	16

(B)

x	y
1	5
2	10
3	15
4	20

(C)

x	y
2	54
3	36
4	27
6	18

(D)

x	y
1	2
2	3
3	4
4	5

(E)

x	y
1	1
2	3
3	5
4	7

x	4	6	8	10
y	16	10.67	8	6.4

2 The table above gives values of a relation for selected values of x. Which of the following defines y in terms of x ?

(A) $y = 1.5x$

(B) $y = x^{-1}$

(C) $y = \dfrac{24}{x}$

(D) $y = \dfrac{48}{x}$

(E) $y = \dfrac{64}{x}$

Hard

3 If y is inversely proportional to x^2, and $y = 16$ when $x = 2$, what is x when $y = \dfrac{1}{2}$?

(A) $8\sqrt{2}$

(B) $4\sqrt{6}$

(C) $\sqrt{2}$

(D) 16

(E) 32

4 If y varies inversely with x and $y = 10$ when $x = 3$, what is the value of x when $y = 8$?

(A) 1.75

(B) 2.75

(C) 3.75

(D) 4.75

(E) 5.75

How to Think Like a Math Genius I

You've now learned the 47 skills that you need for the SAT. The Math Mantras remind you what to do when, what that girl who got an 800 does automatically. In Skills 48 and 49, let's make sure you've memorized the 47 SAT Math Mantras. Cut out the flash cards provided at the end of this book, and drill them until you are ready to teach them. Then do that. Once you're sure you've got 'em, check off the box next to each mantra.

☐ **Skill 1.** When you see variables in the question and numbers in the answers, "Use the Answers."

☐ **Skill 2.** "What is m in terms of p and q" is just a fancy way of saying "solve for m" or "use algebra to get m alone."

☐ **Skill 3.** When you see the word "average" on the SAT, use sum = (average) × (# of items).

☐ **Skill 4.** When you see vertical angles, a linear pair, or a triangle, calculate the measures of all angles.

☐ **Skill 5.** When you see two parallel lines that are crossed by another line, eight angles are formed, and all the bigger-looking angles are equal, and all the smaller-looking angles are equal.

☐ **Skill 6.** When you see a triangle with two equal sides, mark the two opposite angles as equal, and when all sides of a triangle are equal, mark all angles 60°.

☐ **Skill 7.** An exterior angle equals the sum of the two far away interior angles.

☐ **Skills 8 and 9.** Anytime you see a math vocab term, underline it.

☐ **Skill 10.** Don't be intimidated by fancy vocabulary terms.

☐ **Skill 11.** The slope of a line measures its steepness; the steeper the line, the bigger the slope.

☐ **Skill 12.** Parallel lines have equal slopes, like $\frac{2}{3}$ and $\frac{2}{3}$. Perpendicular lines have negative reciprocal slopes, like $\frac{2}{3}$ and $-\frac{3}{2}$. And lines reflected over the x axis or y axis have negative slopes, like $\frac{2}{3}$ and $-\frac{2}{3}$.

☐ **Skill 13.** The key to understanding tables and graphs is to read the headings and the legend if there is one.

☐ **Skill 14.** $f(3)$ means "plug 3 in for x."

☐ **Skill 15.** $f(m) = 9$ means "What did we plug into the equation for x to get a result of 9?"

☐ **Skill 16.** When you see variables in the question and variables in the answer choices, especially for word problems, use "Make It Real."

☐ **Skill 17.** The SAT only expects you to use formulas provided in the question or in the info box at the beginning of the section.

□ **Skill 18.** The area of a donut equals the area of the big guy minus the area of the donut hole.

□ **Skill 19.** 4 boys to 5 girls could also be expressed 5 girls to 9 students. Also a ratio can be a reduced version of the real numbers.

□ **Skill 20.** When you see a proportion on the SAT, cross-multiply.

Here's the question from the Pretest.

Movie	Votes	♥ = 10 votes
Superbad	♥ ♥ ♥ ♥ ♥	
Borat	♥ ❝	
Wedding Crashers	♥ ❝	
Godfather	♥	

48. The table above shows the results of a survey in which 90 high school students voted for their favorite movie. Each student received one vote. According to the graph, how many more students favored *Superbad* than *Borat*?

    (A) 3   (B) 3.5   (C) 35   (D) 39.5   (E) 40

Solution: The legend tells us that each ♥ represents 10 votes. Therefore, *Superbad* received 50 votes and *Borat* received 15, and $50 - 15 = 35$. Remember that half a symbol represents 5 votes, not half a vote.

Correct answer: C

How to Think Like a Math Genius I Drills

Name the skill(s) that you can use, and then solve each question.

Easy

1 If $\frac{3}{12} = \frac{5}{a}$, what is the value of a ?

(A) 60

(B) 40

(C) 30

(D) 20

(E) 14

2 If the average (arithmetic mean) of the perimeters of two shapes is 14, what is the sum of the perimeters of the two shapes?

(A) 0

(B) 7

(C) 14

(D) 21

(E) 28

Medium

3 If two sides of a triangle are equal, which of the following could be the measures of its angles?

(A) 30, 30, 90

(B) 35, 45, 100

(C) 35, 35, 110

(D) 30, 60, 90

(E) 45, 45, 45

4 Five boys on an elevator have an average (arithmetic mean) weight of 120. A sixth boy wants to join them. If the elevator can hold 750 lb, what is the maximum the sixth boy can weigh in order for the group not to exceed the elevator's 750-pound weight limit?

5 If $f(x) = 3x^3$, and $f(b) = 24$, then $b =$

(A) −1

(B) 0

(C) 2

(D) 8

(E) 9

6 A fruit cup contains apple, pear, and banana in the ratio 2 : 3 : 4. If a serving of fruit cup contains 9 pieces of pear, how many total pieces of fruit are in the cup?

7 The function $M(u) = (2u)^2 - k$ expresses the number of songs Simon has memorized this year, where u represents months so far this year and $M(u)$ represents songs memorized. If by the end of June he has memorized 9 songs, what is the value of k ?

(A) 6

(B) 9

(C) 63

(D) 135

(E) 318

Hard

8 If a is a multiple of 3 and b is a multiple of 4, which of the following must be a multiple of 12 ?

   I. ab

  II. $3a + 4b$

  III. $4a + 3b$

(A) I only

(B) III only

(C) I and III

(D) II and III

(E) I, II, and III

9 In the diagram above, what is the value of a in terms of b and c ?

(A) $90 + 4b + c$

(B) $180 - 3b - 2c$

(C) $180 + 2b + c$

(D) $360 - 4b - 2c$

(E) $360 + 3b - c$

10 The average (arithmetic mean) of the bowling scores of a team of m students is 170, and the average of the scores of a class of n students is 182. When the scores of both teams are combined, the average score is 177.5. What is the value of m/n ?

(A) 0.4

(B) 0.6

(C) 0.8

(D) 1

(E) 1.2

How to Think Like a Math Genius II

Learning mantras is like learning martial arts. Practice until they become part of you, until you follow them naturally: when you see a proportion, you cross-multiply; when you see a linear pair, you fill in the angles. . . . This will fundamentally change you as a math student. In fact, after SAT prep, many students begin to like math; they realize that they "get" it, and it stops being intimidating, and becomes easy. I've even seen kids overcome serious math phobias with the Mantras. Your SAT score and probably even your math class grades will go way up.

Here are the rest of the SAT Math Mantras. Check the box next to each one when you have mastered it. Reread the Skill sections if you need to.

☐ **Skill 21.** "Use the Diagram" to estimate an answer. Translate into decimals any answer choices that contain $\sqrt{}$ or π.

☐ **Skill 22.** When a diagram is not drawn to scale, redraw it. And when a picture is described, but not shown, draw it!

☐ **Skill 23.** When you see a right triangle, try $a^2 + b^2 = c^2$.

☐ **Skill 24.** When you see a 30°, 45°, or 60° angle in a right triangle, try using the special right triangles.

☐ **Skill 25.** Similar triangles have sides that are proportional.

☐ **Skill 26.** Translate word problems from English to math.

☐ **Skill 27.** When something can be factored, FOILed, reduced, or simplified, . . . do it.

☐ **Skill 28.** Memorize the laws of exponents.

☐ **Skill 30.** For the equation $y = mx + b$ or $y = ax + b$, m or a is the slope and b is the y intercept.

☐ **Skill 31.** When you see an arrangement question, draw a blank for each position, fill in the # of possibilities to fill each position, and multiply.

☐ **Skill 32.** When an arrangement question mentions a "restriction," fill in the restricted positions first. When it mentions a "team of two," divide your result by 2.

☐ **Skill 33.** When you see "probability," use the equation Probability $= \frac{\text{want}}{\text{total}}$.

☐ **Skill 34.** When you see "median" or "mode," rewrite the data as a list in order.

☐ **Skill 35.** For the equation $y = ax^2 + bx + c$, the a tells whether the U-shaped graph opens up or down, and the c is the y intercept.

☐ **Skill 36.** Logic questions are easy long as you stay focused and do NOT get intimidated.

☐ **Skill 37.** Remainders are what's left over when you use long division.

☐ **Skill 38.** When you see absolute value, look for the less obvious answer.

☐ **Skill 40.** To solve a sequence question, write the next bunch of terms until you have as many as you need or until you see a repeating pattern.

☐ **Skill 41.** "Careless errors are bad mmmkay," so underline all vocabulary words and remember to finish the question.

☐ **Skill 45.** When you see a weird symbol question: (1) relax, (2) remember that no one has seen this symbol before, and (3) follow the directions given in the question.

Here's the question from the Pretest.

49. Ahmed is both the 7th tallest and 7th shortest student in class. If everyone is a different height, how many total students are there in the class?

Solution: Draw a simple diagram. Anytime a picture or a situation is described, draw it (Skill 22). It helps you to see what to do next and to avoid careless errors. Without a diagram, many students answer 14 or 15, but the diagram shows that in height order, Ahmed is the 7th in both directions, so there are 6 students on each side of him. Thus, 6 students on his right plus 6 on the left plus Ahmed equals 13 students total.

Correct answer: 13

How to Think Like a Math Genius II Drills

Name the skill(s) that you can use, and then solve each question.

Easy

1 If $m < 0$, which of the following is greatest?

Ⓐ m

Ⓑ $3m$

Ⓒ $6m$

Ⓓ $9m$

Ⓔ It cannot be determined from the information given.

2 If $p < -1$, which of the following is greatest?

Ⓐ p

Ⓑ $1 + p$

Ⓒ $1 - p$

Ⓓ p^3

Ⓔ $\dfrac{p}{2}$

3 If $m(x) = 2(3x)^2$, what is the value of $m(n)$?

Ⓐ $18\,n^2$

Ⓑ $36\,n^2$

Ⓒ $56\,n^2$

Ⓓ $72\,n^2$

Ⓔ $144\,n^2$

Medium

4 If the Yoga Club has 42 members and the Dungeons and Dragons Live Action Role Playing Club has 25 members and there are 18 students that belong to both clubs, how many people total will be at a joint meeting of both clubs, if all members attend?

Ⓐ 18

Ⓑ 31

Ⓒ 49

Ⓓ 58

Ⓔ 67

5 If 4 less than half a number is equal to thirty percent of the number, what is 3 times the number?

Ⓐ 2

Ⓑ 5

Ⓒ 12

Ⓓ 30

Ⓔ 60

6 For the numbers in the data set {3, 5, 1, 7, 7, 3, 2, p, 1, 3,}, the median is 3 and the only mode is 3. Each of the following could be the value of p EXCEPT

(A) 3
(B) 4
(C) 5
(D) 6
(E) 7

Hard

7 Set M consists of m members, and set P consists of p members. And r represents the number of members that belong to both set M and set P. If set Z consists only of members who belong to either set M or set P, but not both, which of the following could represent the number of members of set Z ?

(A) $m + p - r$
(B) $m + p - 2r$
(C) $m - p - r$
(D) $m - p + 2r$
(E) $m + p$

8 If each of the five finalists in the world SAT Math Olympics will face each of the others in head-to-head competition, how many of these one-on-one matches will be played?

9 The dartboard shown above has a small circle, with radius 3.5, inside a larger circle, with radius 5. When Matty randomly throws a dart at the board, which of the following is closest to the probability that it will land in the shaded region?

(A) $\frac{1}{12}$
(B) $\frac{1}{6}$
(C) $\frac{1}{2}$
(D) $\frac{3}{4}$
(E) $\frac{5}{6}$

10 If $|x - 3| = 4$ and $|y + 2| = 3$, what is the greatest possible value for $x - y$?

(A) -8
(B) -2
(C) 0
(D) 6
(E) 12

Brian's Friday Night Spiel: Recommendations for the Days Preceding the Test

Studies show that sleeping and eating healthfully two days before the test (or any important event) is as important as sleeping and eating healthfully the night before. So on Thursday night eat a healthy dinner and go to bed early—not so early that you're lying in bed at 7:00 p.m. tense, hungry, and staring at the cracks in the ceiling, but normal early, maybe 10:00 p.m.

Friday, have a normal day, no need to cram or stress. If you have completed this book and one or more timed practice tests, you are ready. Go to school, play sports or whatever you do after school, have a healthy dinner, and do something fun and relaxing. Don't hang out with anyone who stresses you out or obsesses over the test. Read, play a game, or watch a funny movie—I recommend *Fletch*, *Wedding Crashers*, or *40-Year-Old Virgin*—and go to bed at a sensible time. If you live in a household where, in the morning, everyone roams the house, screaming for a clean shirt and car keys, then gather your snack, drink, admission ticket, ID, pencils, watch, and calculator in the evening.

You should eat breakfast and pack a snack because it's a long day and you have to feed the brain. I recommend a cheese sandwich or two Luna bars, they are high in protein and not too high in sugar, good brain food. If you need an extra special boost, in India some people take a few drops of almond oil on the morning of a test.

Let's take a look at the question from the Pretest.

50. The night before the SAT you should

(A) Eat 2 pounds of pasta for a runner's endurance energy.
(B) Eat two whole live lobsters for omega-3 fatty acids.
(C) Host a huge pre-SAT party.
(D) Stay up until 2 a.m. drilling the Pythagorean theorem.
(E) Relax and sleep well.

Solution: Relax and sleep well, you are prepared. Now, go get 'em!

Correct answer: E

Test Day Checklist	
2 Protein bars	#2 Pencils
Beverage	Calculator
Your admission ticket	A watch (to keep track of time)
Photo ID (driver's license, school ID, or passport)	

Brian's Friday Night Spiel: Recommendations for the Days Preceding the Test Drills

Here is your last drill section. Your last assignment is to be able to stay relaxed, even under pressure. So here is a little tool that you can use anytime, even during the test.

In the 1970s Herbert Benson, a researcher at Harvard Medical School, published work on what he called the *relaxation response*, a physiological response where the body and mind relax. Benson reported that the relaxation response was triggered by practicing 20 minutes of a concentration exercise, basically meditation. Apparently, Yale, always in competition with Harvard, decided to one-up them. "We need a way to trigger the relaxation response but in less than Benson's 20 minutes!" they might have bemoaned. They researched, and they tried as hard as they could to relax; it was quite stressful. Finally, someone came up with the following goofy exercise. And it is goofy, but the thing is, it works! It totally works. Do it and you'll see.

Follow these steps:

❶ Breathing through your nose, become aware of your breath.
❷ Relax your shoulders and face.
❸ Allow your exhale to be longer than your inhale.
❹ Now, drop your shoulders and head and smile and then bring your head back up.
❺ Repeat: drop your shoulders and head and smile, and then bring your head back up.
❻ Notice how you feel.

That's it! Anytime you feel stressed, even during the test, try this very simple exercise to trigger your "relaxation response."

Score is tied: Yale, 1. Harvard, 1.

Hello Harvard . . . How to Break 700

Sucking all the marrow out of life doesn't mean choking on the bone.
John Keating, *Dead Poets Society* (Touchstone Pictures, 1989)

Want to break 700? Here are the six steps to do it.

But first you have to promise me that you are doing this because you want to, and not out of some obsessive, sleep doesn't matter, gotta please my parents, if I don't go to Tufts I'm nothing, misunderstanding. Strive to do well, yes. Also stay balanced. Sleep. Eat well. Exercise. Be true to yourself. Be brave. Be honest. Be relaxed. Breathe. And from that place, give it all that you got . . . .

❶ Make sure you understand all 50 Skills. Don't just look at them and say, "Yeah, I can do that." Practice. Do the drills. Make sure you can get every question correct on every Skill. If you can't, reread the section, read the solutions, and keep redoing the drills until they make perfect sense. Then teach them to a friend.

❷ Memorize the careless errors to avoid. Keep them in mind as you drill until avoiding careless errors becomes second-nature.

❸ Master Posttests I and II (Posttest II is on the CD-ROM). Take each test, read the solutions, and redo any questions that you missed.

❹ Once you've mastered Posttests I and II, take Posttest III (CD-ROM), which consists of 50 very hard questions. Take the test, read the solutions, and redo any questions that you missed. When you master these 50 very challenging questions, you are ready to break 700!

❺ Then take **at least** one timed SAT (see "Now What?" page 118). Score and review the test. Keep taking timed practice tests until you confidently and consistently break 700.

❻ Finally, remember the words of quantum physics and of Jedi Master Yoda, "Do, or do not. There is no try." (*Star Wars Episode V: The Empire Strikes Back*, 20th Century Fox, 1980)

Easy, Medium, Hard, and Guessing Revisited

Let's revisit what I told you way back at the beginning of the book. It will probably make even more sense now.

The SAT is not graded like a math test at school. To get a 500, the average score for kids across the country, you need to get about half the questions correct. To get a 600, the average score for admission to schools like Goucher and University of Vermont, you need about 70% correct. And for a beautiful 700 on the SAT, the average for kids who got into Georgetown, U.C. Berkeley, Emory, and Wesleyan, you must answer 89% of the questions correctly.

Use this info to determine how many questions you need to answer on the SAT. Remember that on the SAT, in each section, the first third of the questions are "easy," the middle bunch are "medium," and a little less than the last third are "hard." In other words, of 20 questions, perhaps 7 are easy, 8 are medium, and 5 are hard. Also some math sections are broken up into two parts, #1–8 and #9–18, each part organized easiest to hardest. You can always recognize these two-part sections because #9–18 are student-produced response questions, the type without answer choices.

Knowing this order of difficulty is important because if you need only half correct or 70% correct, don't rush through the easies and mediums just to get to the hard ones. All questions are worth the same amount. Not rushing is the best way to avoid careless errors. In school you might need to finish tests in order to do well, here you do not. **You only need to get to the very hardest questions if you are shooting for 700+.**

Guessing? Don't randomly guess, but if you are unsure of a question, sometimes you can get it correct by the process of elimination. When you can confidently eliminate at least one answer choice, take an educated guess. If you get it right, you gain four times as much as you lose if it's wrong. So educated guesses pay off. Of course, now that you've completed this book, you'll barely need to guess! When you feel stumped, take another look and ask yourself, "Which Math Mantra/Skill can I use?"

Now What?

Take the Posttest. Check your answers and review the Skills for any questions that were difficult. Then take Posttest II found on the CD-ROM that came with this book. If you are shooting for 700+, take Posttest III (also on the CD-ROM), which contains 50 "hard" questions.

After you have completed the Posttests, go to your guidance office and pick up the free packet entitled "SAT Preparation Booklet: Get Ready for the SAT," which contains a full practice test with answers and scoring instructions. Or you can download a free test at www.collegeboard.com.

Take the test as a dress rehearsal; get up early on a Saturday, time it, use the answer sheets, and fill in the ovals. If you have competed this book, you will find that you are very well prepared. Correct and score the test, and review whatever you got wrong. Figure out which SAT Math Mantras you could have used to get them right.

If you have some time, purchase *The Official SAT Study Guide*, published by The College Board. It contains eight practice tests. Take one practice test per week as a dress rehearsal. Take it when you are relaxed and focused. We want only your best work. Less than that will earn you a lower score than you are capable of and is bad for morale. Score each test and review whatever you got wrong. Figure out which SAT Math Mantras you could have used to get them right.

Now, you are ready, you beautiful SAT monster. Go get'em!

Posttest I

This posttest contains 50 questions that review our 50 Skills. Take the test. Then check your answers and review the Skills for any questions that were difficult.

❶ If $8^{x+1} = 2^{x+7}$, what is the value of x ?

Ⓐ 1
Ⓑ 2
Ⓒ 3
Ⓓ 4
Ⓔ 5

❷ If $2m = 5n$ and $5n = 6p$, what is m in terms of p ?

Ⓐ 5p
Ⓑ 3p
Ⓒ 2.9p
Ⓓ 2.4p
Ⓔ p

❸ On 10 tests, a student calculated her test average to be 82. However, she discovered that 2 of the grades were recorded incorrectly. The number 85 was entered as 80, and the number 99 was entered as 90. To the nearest whole number, what is the correct average for her 10 grades?

Ⓐ 81
Ⓑ 82
Ⓒ 83
Ⓓ 84
Ⓔ 85

❹ In the figure above, what is the value of x ?

Note: Figure not drawn to scale.

❺ In the figure above, $m \parallel n$. If $x = 53$, what is the value of y ?

Ⓐ 27
Ⓑ 53
Ⓒ 90
Ⓓ 127
Ⓔ 180

Note: Figure not drawn to scale.

6 If $MN = ON$ in the figure above, and $b = 160$, what is the value of c ?

(A) 5

(B) 10

(C) 20

(D) 30

(E) 80

7 In the figure above, what is the value of x ?

8 If 3 consecutive even numbers have a sum of 42, what is the smallest number?

9 If $12 < x < 36$, and 36 is the lowest number that is a multiple of 4, 12, and x, what is the value for x ?

10 In an xy coordinate plane, two lines may intersect at how many ordered pairs (x, y) ?

  I. 0

 II. 1

III. 2

(A) I only

(B) III only

(C) I and II

(D) II and III

(E) I, II, and III

11 What is the slope of the line through the points $(2, 3)$ and $(-1, 0)$?

(A) -1

(B) 0

(C) 1

(D) 3

(E) Undefined

12 If the line through the points $(-1, 3)$ and $(-2, p)$ is parallel to the line $y = 3x - 3$, what is the value of p ?

(A) -2

(B) -1

(C) 0

(D) 1

(E) 2

Spice Girl	Votes
Scary	♥ ♥ ♥ ♥ ❜
Baby	♥ ♥
Ginger	♥ ♥
Posh	♥ ♥ ♥
Sporty	♥ ♥ ♥ ♥

♥ = 20 votes

13 The table above shows the results of a survey in which 310 high school students voted for their favorite Spice Girl. Each student received one vote. According to the graph, how many more students favored Scary Spice than Posh Spice?

(A) 1.5

(B) 15

(C) 20

(D) 25

(E) 30

14 If $f(x) = -3x^2 - 2$, what is the value of $f(-1)$?

(A) -6

(B) -5

(C) 1

(D) 5

(E) 6

x	$f(x)$
0	2
1	3
2	6
3	11

15 The table above shows the values of the quadratic function f for selected values of x. Which of the following defines f ?

(A) $f(x) = x^2 + 1$

(B) $f(x) = x^2 + 2$

(C) $f(x) = 3x^2 - 2$

(D) $f(x) = 3x^2 - 1$

(E) $f(x) = 3x^2 + 1$

16 If t is a negative number, which of the following must be a positive number?

(A) $t + 1$

(B) $t + 2$

(C) $3 - t$

(D) $\dfrac{t}{3}$

(E) $3t$

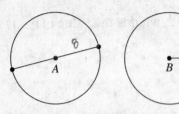

Note: Figure not drawn to scale.

17 For the circles above, the diameter of circle A is 16 and the radius of circle B is half the diameter of circle A. What is the area of circle B?

Ⓐ 8

Ⓑ 16π

Ⓒ 24π

Ⓓ 64π

Ⓔ 160π

18 In the figure above, the perimeter of square BCDF is 24, DE = 4, and AB = 12. What is the perimeter of the shaded region?

Ⓐ 28

Ⓑ 43

Ⓒ 56

Ⓓ 68

Ⓔ 82

19 The ratio 1.4 to 2 is equal to which of the following?

Ⓐ 1 to 4

Ⓑ 14 to 2

Ⓒ 10 to 7

Ⓓ 7 to 10

Ⓔ 7 to 100

20 A scale model of a certain airplane is $\frac{3}{35}$ the height of the actual airplane. If the scale is 3.5 inches tall, what is the height of the actual plane?

Ⓐ $38\frac{4}{5}$

Ⓑ 40

Ⓒ $40\frac{5}{6}$

Ⓓ 42

Ⓔ $57\frac{5}{8}$

21 The rectangular solid above has edges of length 20, 8, and 4. If point M (not shown) is the midpoint of segment AB, what is the length of MD?

Ⓐ $4\sqrt{2}$

Ⓑ $3\sqrt{10}$

Ⓒ $6\sqrt{5}$

Ⓓ $2\sqrt{65}$

Ⓔ $8\sqrt{5}$

22 $ABED$ is a square with sides of length 6. If point C is the midpoint of ED, what is the perimeter of $ABCD$?

Ⓐ 18

Ⓑ $15 + 3\sqrt{5}$

Ⓒ $18 + 3\sqrt{5}$

Ⓓ $22 + 3\sqrt{5}$

Ⓔ 36

Note: Figure not drawn to scale.

23 In the right triangle above, what is the value of p?

Ⓐ 8

Ⓑ 16

Ⓒ 32

Ⓓ 48

Ⓔ 64

24 In right triangle MNO (not shown), the measure of MN is 6 and the measure of NO is 3. Which of the following could be the measure of OM?

Ⓐ 3

Ⓑ $3\sqrt{3}$

Ⓒ $4\sqrt{3}$

Ⓓ $5\sqrt{3}$

Ⓔ 9

25 In the isosceles triangle *MNO* above, a segment is drawn between midpoints *A* and *B* of the two congruent sides. All the following are true EXCEPT

Ⓐ $\angle M \cong \angle O$

Ⓑ $\angle B \cong \angle A$

Ⓒ $\triangle MNO \sim \triangle BNA$

Ⓓ $BA = MO$

Ⓔ $BN = NA$

26 When the product of 3 and a number is increased by 5, the result is 350. What is the number?

27 If $x = p(p - 3)$, then $x + 2 =$

Ⓐ $p^2 - 3p$

Ⓑ $p^2 + 3$

Ⓒ $p^2 - 3p + 2$

Ⓓ $p^2 + 3p + 2$

Ⓔ $p^2 + 3p$

28 What is the product of $3bm^4$ and $2b^4$?

Ⓐ $5mb^8$

Ⓑ $6mb^8$

Ⓒ $6m^4b^4$

Ⓓ $5m^4b^5$

Ⓔ $6m^4b^5$

29 If $a^{-3} = b^{-9}$, what is the value of *a* when $b = 2$?

Ⓐ -2

Ⓑ 0

Ⓒ 2

Ⓓ 4

Ⓔ 8

30 The figure above shows the graph of the line $y = ax + b$. Which of the following best represents the graph of $y = 3ax + b$?

(A)

(B)

(C)

(D)

(E)

31 For a fund-raiser, the yoga club is selling tee-shirts with a choice of two slogans, "Ooommmm" or "Bend me!" Each shirt is available in lavender or peach and in small, medium, or large. How many different types of shirts are available?

32 Kate, Jack, Sawyer, Walt, and Hugo are at the beach. If a team of two people will hike to the caves, how many different such pairs are possible?

$$\{3, 4, 5, 6, 7, 8\}$$

33 What is the probability of randomly choosing a prime number from the set above?

34 If $2m - 2$, $m + 3$, and $3m - 4$ are all integers and $m + 3$ is the median of these integers, which of the following could be a value for m?

(A) 2
(B) 4
(C) 6
(D) 8
(E) 10

35 If m is a positive constant and $n = 0$, which of the following could be the graph of $y = mx^2 + 3x + n$?

Ⓐ

Ⓑ

Ⓒ

Ⓓ

Ⓔ

36 If all children in the Lederman family are terrific, which of the following statements must be true?

Ⓐ All terrific children are Ledermans.

Ⓑ All children not in the Lederman family are not terrific.

Ⓒ No children who are not terrific are in the Lederman family.

Ⓓ Everyone in the Lederman family who is terrific is a child.

Ⓔ There are four terrific children in the Lederman family.

37 Which of the following could be the remainders when four consecutive odd integers are each divided by 3 ?

Ⓐ 1, 3, 5, 0

Ⓑ 1, 2, 3, 4

Ⓒ 0, 1, 2, 3

Ⓓ 0, 2, 1, 0

Ⓔ 0, 1, 2, 0

38 Which of the following are solutions to $|x - 2| = 6$?

I. 8

II. −4

III. −3

Ⓐ I only

Ⓑ II only

Ⓒ I and II

Ⓓ I and III

Ⓔ I, II, and III

6, 10, 18, 34, . . .

39 In the sequence above, the first term is 6, and every number after the first is found by subtracting 1 and then doubling the result. What is the 7th term in the sequence?

Ⓐ 257
Ⓑ 258
Ⓒ 259
Ⓓ 260
Ⓔ 261

6, 10, 14, 18, . . .

40 In the sequence above, the first term is 6, and every number after the first is found by adding 4 to the preceding term. What is the 57th term in the sequence?

Ⓐ 230
Ⓑ 232
Ⓒ 234
Ⓓ 235
Ⓔ 239

41 When $x = -2$, which of the following is equivalent to $x(2s^2 - 2)$?

Ⓐ $-4s^2 + 4$
Ⓑ $-4s^2 - 4$
Ⓒ $4s^2 - 4$
Ⓓ $4s^2 + 4$
Ⓔ $s^2 - 4$

42 If $x = 2$, then which of the following is equivalent to $(y - x)^2$?

Ⓐ $y - 2$
Ⓑ $y^2 + 4$
Ⓒ $y^2 + 2y + 4$
Ⓓ $y^2 + 4y + 4$
Ⓔ $y^2 - 4y + 4$

43 If point N on the number line above represents -8, and point M (not shown) is between N and -4, which of the following could be represented by point M ?

Ⓐ 8
Ⓑ 4
Ⓒ 0
Ⓓ -5
Ⓔ -8

44 The graph of g(x) is shown above. Which of the following equations represents all the points of g(x) shifted 1 unit down?

Ⓐ $y = g(x) + 1$
Ⓑ $y = g(x + 1)$
Ⓒ $y = g(x - 1)$
Ⓓ $y = g(x) - 1$
Ⓔ $y = g(x)$

45. Let $d\,\boxed{\begin{array}{cc} a & b \\ & c \end{array}}$ be defined as $d\,\boxed{\begin{array}{cc} a & b \\ & c \end{array}} = ac + db$ for all integers a, b, c, and d. What is the value of $4\,\boxed{\begin{array}{cc} 3 & 5 \\ & 6 \end{array}}$?

46. If y is directly proportional to x, and $y = 21$ when $x = 4$, what is x when $y = 35$?

47. If y is inversely proportional to x^2, and $y = \frac{1}{2}$ when $x = 2$, what is x when $y = \frac{1}{8}$?

    Ⓐ 4

    Ⓑ 2

    Ⓒ 1

    Ⓓ $\frac{1}{2}$

    Ⓔ $\frac{1}{16}$

48. In a basket of orange and purple crayons, the ratio of orange crayons to purple crayons is 2 to 3. Which of the following could be the total number of crayons in the basket?

    Ⓐ 2

    Ⓑ 6

    Ⓒ 14

    Ⓓ 15

    Ⓔ 27

$$\{4, 5, 6, 7, 8, 9\}$$

49. What is the probability of randomly choosing an odd prime number from the set above?

50. The morning of the test you should

    Ⓐ Drink 4 Jolt colas to be wide awake.

    Ⓑ Feed your brain with a tall stack of flapjacks, a side of pork, and six potatoes.

    Ⓒ Run a few miles.

    Ⓓ Take a full 4-hour timed practice test.

    Ⓔ Have a normal healthy breakfast.

Solutions

Pretest

Solutions are on each Skill page.

Skill 1 (page 11)

Use the Answers

1. **C** You can answer this question quickly and easily by using simple algebra and solving for x. If, however, that is difficult or daunting, "Use the Answers." Just plug each choice in to see which one makes the equation work. Choice C is correct: $2(10) - 3 = 17$.

2. **E** You can answer this question, like #1 above, by using algebra and solving for p. Or you can just "Use the Answers." Plug each choice in to see which one makes the equation work. Choice E is correct: $4(3) + 2 < 15$.

3. **E** You can answer this question by using algebra and solving for j, or just "Use the Answers." Plug each choice in to see which one makes the equation work. Choice E is correct: $\frac{3+1}{2^3} = \frac{4}{8} = \frac{1}{2}$.

4. **D** You can answer this question by using algebra and solving for n, or just "Use the Answers." Plug each choice in to see which one makes the equation work. Choice D is correct: $|3 - 6|$ equals 3 which is less than 4. ($|3 - 6|$ means the absolute value of $3 - 6$, which is just fancy language for subtract $3 - 6$ and make the answer positive. More on this in Skill 38.)

5. **A** You can answer this question by using algebra and solving for t; however, this "medium" difficulty question requires more involved algebra. "Use the Answers" makes the question EASY! Just plug each choice in to see which one makes the equation work. Choice A is correct since

$$\sqrt{\frac{-2(-54)}{3}} = \sqrt{\frac{108}{3}} = \sqrt{36} = 6$$

6. **E** "Use the Answers," makes this easy. Just plug the choices in for u in the equation. Each choice yields a result (which represents production cost) less than \$7300. So 4 is the highest and thus the correct answer. This question is rated "hard" because it involves functions, fractions, and variables in the exponents; difficult for many students, but easy for you with "Use the Answers."

Skill 2 (page 13)

"What Is P in Terms of F?"

1. **D** What is R in terms of D and T?" means "solve for R." In other words, get R alone.

   $D = RT$ divide both sides by T

   $\frac{D}{T} = R$

2. **B** "What is m in terms of p?" means "solve for m, get m alone." Since $3m = 2n = 4p$, we can say

   $3m = 4p$ divide both sides by 3

   $m = \frac{4p}{3}$

3. **D** "What is $b - 1$ in terms of x and k?" means solve for $b - 1$, get it alone. This is unusual. Your math teacher never asks for $b - 1$, she just asks for b. But the SAT is weird and asks for $b - 1$. So we simply solve for $b - 1$, no biggie.

   $x + 3(b - 1) = k$ subtract x from both sides

   $3(b - 1) = k - x$ divide both sides by 3

   $b - 1 = \frac{k - x}{3}$

4. **E** "What does p^{-1} equal in terms of q?" means solve for p^{-1}. Your math teacher would never ask you to solve for p^{-1}, but the SAT does. No problem, just solve for p^{-1}, get it alone.

   $5p^3q^{-2} = 25p^2$ divide both sides by p^2

   $5pq^{-2} = 25$ divide both sides by $5q^{-2}$

   $p = \frac{5}{q^{-2}} = 5q^2$ the question asks for p^{-1}, so just bring both sides to the -1 power

   $p^{-1} = \frac{1}{5q^2}$

Skill 3 (page 15)

"Mean" Means Average

1. **E** Set up the average formula: $(m + 4m)/2 = 30$. Then use algebra to solve for m or "Use the Answers" to see which one works.

2. **E** Most kids get this one wrong, but with the sum formula it's easy! Set up the sum formula: Sum $= (k)(21)$. Therefore, Sum $= 21k$. EASY!

3. **D** Set up the sum formula: $(m + n) = 7 \times 2$. Thus, $m + n$ equals 14. Then use the sum formula for the second set of data: $(m + n + p) = 11 \times 3$. So their sum is 33. Since $m + n + p$ equals 33 and $m + n$ equals 14, p must equal $33 - 14 = 19$.

4. **D** This question is a medium because many people fear fractions. Don't! They are easy, you can even turn them into decimals on your calculator if you don't like them (just divide the top number by the bottom number). With the average formula this question is very easy. Average = sum / # items. So average = 9/2.

5. **C** Set up the sum formula to find the sum for each class, then add the sums and divide by the total number of students in the classes to arrive at the combined average:
$$\frac{(80)(20) + (92)(30)}{20 + 30} = 87.2$$

6. **130** This question follows our strategy perfectly. If the average of m, n, o, and p is 55, then their sum is $55 \times 4 = 220$; and if m, n, o, p, and q average to 70, then their sum is $70 \times 5 = 350$. Therefore the value of q is the difference between the sums: $350 - 220 = 130$.

7. **25** If 5 judges average 7, then using our sum formula, sum = average $\times$ # items, the sum is 35. If we want one judge's number to be as big as possible, then we want the other judges' numbers to be as low as possible. Since they must be "different integers," the first 4 numbers would be 1, 2, 3, 4, which are the lowest different positive integers. These numbers add up to 10, so we have $35 - 10 = 25$. The last judge can give a whopping score of 25.

Skill 4 (page 17)

The 6-Minute Abs of Geometry: Angles

1. **C** This question uses two of our eight strategies. As soon as you see a linear pair of angles, determine the measure of the unknown angle in the pair. So the angle next to 153° must be $180 - 153 = 27°$. Now we have two of three angles in a triangle which must add up to 180, so the third must be $180 - 80 - 27 = 73$.

2. **B** This is essentially the same question as #1 above. But notice that this figure is not drawn to scale. Whenever this happens, just redraw it roughly to scale. This one is very easy. The angle next to 80° must be $180 - 80 = 100$. Now we have two of three angles in a triangle which must add up to 180°, so the third must be $180 - 100 - 25 = 55$.

3. **C** Mark $y = 60$ into the figure, and as soon as you see a linear pair, solve the other angle, which in this case equals $180 - 60 = 120$. Now we have 4 of the 5 angles of a five-sided figure. A five-sided figure has 540°, so 540 minus the other angles equals the measure of angle z. $z = 540 - 120 - 133 - 139 - 64 = 84$.

4. **30** Use the smaller triangle to determine x ($2x + 75 + 45 = 180$, so $x = 30$). Then use x to solve for the angles in the other triangle:
$120 + 30 + z = 180$
$150 + z = 180$
$z = 30$

5. **E** The two angles form a linear pair, so $2m + 3n = 180$. We need "n in terms of m," so we use algebra to solve for n:

$2m + 3n = 180$	subtract $2m$
$3n = 180 - 2m$	divide by 3
$n = \frac{180 - 2m}{3}$	

Skill 5 (page 1)

The 6-Minute Abs of Geometry: Parallel Lines

1. **C** Easy! In a pair of parallel lines there are only two kinds of angles, big and little, and

the two add up to 180. Since $y = 45$, $x = 180 – 45 = 135$.

2. **D** Parallel lines cut by a transversal make 2 kinds of angles, big and little. Clearly x is little and z is big. If $x = 66$, then $z = 180 – 66 = 114$.

3. **A** First, mark the info that is given in the question into the diagram. That always helps to make the question simpler and usually shows which of our geometry strategies to use. Then use vertical angles, linear pairs, triangles, etc. to calculate the measures of any other angles that you can. The vertical angle to z is 40, and the linear pair to x is 50, so now we have two angles of the triangle. $180 – 50 – 40 = 90$, so the linear pair of y is 90 and is therefore $y = 180 – 90 = 90$.

4. **B** Mark the info from the question into the diagram. Then mark all other angles that you can determine. Now x and y are a linear pair, so $x + y = 180$ and $x = 180 – 95 = 85$. Since the figure is not drawn to scale, you can resketch it to scale. When you do this, you notice that if z and x are both less than 90, the lines cannot be parallel—they are heading toward each other and will intersect. Only choice B is true.

5. **E** Use the strategies. Mark $x = 22$. Therefore, in the triangle, the missing angle is $180 – 108 – 22 = 50$. And in the pair of parallel lines y is a big, not a little, angle; thus it equals $180 – 50 = 130$.

Skill 6 (page 2)

The 6-Minute Abs of Geometry: Triangles

1. **D** As soon as you see an equilateral triangle, mark each angle 60°. Then since r forms a linear pair with 60° angle *UEQ*, $r = 180 – 60 = 120$.

2. **B** As soon as you know that two sides in a triangle are equal, you know that the two angles opposite the two sides are also equal.

Therefore, $a = c$. Now $b = 43$, and $a + c + 43 = 180$, so $a + c = 137$. Since a equals c, a is half of 137, which equals 68.5.

3. **D** Mark info from the question into the diagram. Since $AC = AB = 7$ and the perimeter is 21, CB must also equal 7 and the triangle is equilateral. Therefore, all angles of the triangle are 60s.

4. **C** Area = 0.5(base)(height)
$$72 = 0.5(12)(MN)$$
So $MN = 12$ and the triangle is isosceles. Therefore, the base angles are equal. Since angle M is 90°, the base angles must add up to $180 – 90 = 90$, and since they are equal, they are 45° each.

Skill 7 (page 23)

The Final 6-Minute Abs of Geometry

1. **90** We've seen this question before, but now we have even more Skills to answer it. Look for our strategies. Are there vertical angles we can use? No. Linear pairs? Maybe. Triangles? Shaboom! $2x + 75 + 45 = 180$, use algebra to get $x = 30$ and plug that into the other triangle. So $30 + 30 + y = 180$. Use algebra to get $y = 120$. Also Skill 7 gives us a shortcut here since y is an exterior angle to the first triangle and must equal $45 + 75$. So, $y – x = 120 – 30 = 90$.

2. **125** First, label all info that is given in the question into the diagram. Since the measure of $\angle AEB$ is 70, $\angle DEC$ must also be 70 since they are vertical angles. Then $\angle BEC$ makes a linear pair with $\angle AEB$ and must be $180 – 70 = 110$. If segment EF (not shown) bisects $\angle BEC$, then $\angle FEC$ is 55, half of 110. So $\angle FED$ equals $55 + 70 = 125$.

3. **D** The vertical angle of x in the triangle is 71, so the other two angles of the triangle add up to $180 – 71 = 109$. Each of these angles makes a linear pair with y and z, respectively. So these two angles plus y and z make two linear pairs and equal 2(180). Therefore, $109 + y + z = 360$. So use algebra to get $y + z$ alone. In math class this would be unusual. You teacher

usually wants you to solve for just y or just z, but sometimes the SAT asks for $y + z$, so we solve for that. No problem. $y + z = 360 - 109 = 251$.

4. **A** The dotted lines form a small triangle inside the larger triangle. Since the dotted lines bisect angles x and y, the angles of this triangle are z, $\frac{1}{2}y$, $\frac{1}{2}x$. So $z + \frac{1}{2}y + \frac{1}{2}x = 180$. "What is the value of z?" means

   solve for z. So $z = 180 - \frac{1}{2}y - \frac{1}{2}x$. This does not initially seem to match any answers, but

   $180 - \frac{1}{2}y - \frac{1}{2}x - = 180 - 0.5(x + y)$.

Skill 8 (page 25)

Math Vocab

1. **5** This question simply tests whether you know the words "consecutive" and "integer." Many students do not and wind up intimidated and having to skip this very easy question. Since you know what these two words mean, use simple trial and error to solve this question. $4 + 5 = 9$.

2. **C** Most people know that since $3^2 = 9$, there is at least one answer to this question. But the term "different" is the keyword here. It is the tipoff that perhaps there is more than one answer. That should be enough to jog your brain to realize that $(-3)^2 = 9$ also. So there are two possible answers to the question, 3 and -3.

3. **E** Lots of students don't know the term "units digit" and get this wrong; since you know, it's easy. Just list the possibilities: 3, 13, 23, 33, 43, 53, 63, 73, 83, 93.

4. **31** This question intimidates many people. I know so many students who would immediately say, "I have no chance," and move on. I think that this is something the SAT is testing: can you be intimidated? Shout with me now, "NO WAY!" So once we're done with that, this is easy. Just list a bunch of prime numbers: 2, 3, 5, 7, 9, 11, 13, 17, 19, 23, 27, 29, 31 and look for two in a row (consecutive) that add up to 60. So

$29 + 31 = 60$. Cake, if you stay relaxed, focused, and confident.

5. **C** Probably best to just find the 2 numbers. If that seems difficult, "Use the Answers" as hints, that is try -12 and -14. The two numbers are indeed -12 and -14, so I and III are true. II is a trick that the SAT tried and that we can totally predict. -12 might seem less than -14, since 12 is less than 14, but the bigger the negative number, the smaller it is; like the more you owe, the bigger the debt. This sort of trick is discussed more in Skill 43.

6. **8** There are 11 positive integers less than the number 12. How many of these are consecutive odd prime numbers? List the prime numbers that are less than 12: 2, 3, 5, 7, 11. Of these numbers, 3, 5, and 7 **are** consecutive odd numbers, so $11 - 3 = 8$ **are not**.

Skill 9 (page 27)

More Math Vocab

Answer to Brian's Math Magic Trick #1—Multiples: You said carrot. How did I guess your vegetable? Check out my website for answers: www.BrianLeaf.com/carrot

1. **E** List the factors of 120, or better yet "Use the Answers." Just divide 120 by each answer choice. If the number goes into 120 evenly (without a remainder), then it is a factor. And 7 is not a factor, since $120 \div 7 = 17.14$.

2. **D** This question tests if you know the terms "odd" and "factor." Once you do, this is a simple "Use the Answers" type question. Try each answer. Choice A does not work because 2 is not an odd number. Then to test each of the other choices, simply divide 114 by the number. If it goes in evenly, which means you get an integer (no decimal or fraction), then it is a factor. For example, $114 \div 55 = 2.07$, and therefore 55 is not a factor of 114. Choice D is correct since $114 \div 57 = 2$.

3. **E** This question simply asks you to factor 48 and count how many factors there are.

To factor a number, make a list of pairs, as shown below.

1 2 3 4 6 8 12 16 24 48

When you reach 6 × 8, you know that you have them all since only 7, which does not go into 48, is between 6 and 8. Finding factors systematically like this is far better than randomly jotting down numbers. This is true for any SAT math question. Systematic and organized is better than scattered and random. It avoids careless errors, allows you to look back at your work, and helps you make the leap to the next step needed on a complicated question.

4. **B** To complete this question, we factor 48 just as we did above. However, this time we circle any prime numbers in the list. The numbers 2 and 3 are the only prime numbers in the list. Then we write the list of the factors for 100: 1, 2, 4, 5, 10, 20, 25, 50, 100. Of the prime factors of 48, only 2 is also a factor of 100. So set P has 1 member.

5. **D** This question could be difficult, but "Use the Answers" makes it easy! Just test each answer choice by dividing it by 10, 12, and 15. Now 60 is the lowest number on the list that is divisible by 10, 12, and 15. Notice that several other answers work also, but 60 is the lowest. Make sure to finish the question and try all choices!

6. **E** Just try numbers for a, b, and c. This is called "Make It Real" and is discussed more in Skill 16. Let's say $a = 3$, $b = 5$, and $c = 7$. Then $ab^2c = (3)(5)^2(7) = 525$. The long way to do this question is to list the factors of 525: 1, 3, 5, 7, 15, 21, 25, 35, 75, 105, 175, 525. The shortcut is to notice that since a, b, and c are prime, the factors will be 1, a, b, c, ab, ac, bc, b^2, ab^2, cb^2, abc, and ab^2c.

Skill 10 (page 29)

Fancy Math Vocab

1. **E** Don't be intimidated by "xy coordinate plane," it's just the usual grid we use. Same for "ordered pairs," they are just normal (x, y)

points. Draw a sketch. Two circles might intersect in one point, two points, or not at all.

2. **D** Use trial and error. Now x and y must be positive, so start with $x = 1$ (which is the lowest positive integer). If $x = 1$, then $y = 1, 2,$ or 3. If $x = 2$, then $y = 1$ or 2. If $x = 3$, then $y = 1$. And that's it since y must be positive and cannot equal 0, and $x + y < 5$. So there are 6 ordered pairs.

3. **A** The "Cartesian plane," like the xy coordinate plane, is just another name for the normal grid that we always graph on. Since the two lines intersect at (3, 4), just plug this point into each of equations to solve for a and b. (Skill 30 preview: when you have a point and an equation, plug the point into the equation.)

$$y = 2x - b \qquad y = ax + \frac{11}{2}$$
$$4 = 2(3) - b \qquad 4 = a(3) + \frac{11}{2}$$
$$2 = b \qquad -1.5 = 3a$$
$$\qquad\qquad -0.5 = a$$

So $(a)(b) = (-0.5)(2) = -1$.

4. **A** Simply test each point in the equation to see which one works. Point A has coordinates $(-3, 4)$, so $(-3)^2 = 4 + 5$, which works.

5. **B** Ordered pairs (0, 0), (0, 1), (1, 0), (−1, 0), and (0, −1) work.

Skill 11 (page 31)

Slaloming Slope I

1. **B** Plug the two points into the slope equation.
$$\frac{y - y}{x - x} = \frac{-4 - a}{-2 - 3} = \frac{-4 - a}{-5} = \frac{3}{5}$$

Once you have $\frac{-4 - a}{-5} = \frac{3}{5}$, you can simply "Use the Answers" and try each answer choice to see which one makes the equation work. You could also cross-multiply (see Skill 20).

2. **B** This question is exactly like Question 1. You are given 2 points, and you simply plug them into the slope formula. The only twist is that the question refers to the origin as one of the two points so you have to know that "origin" means

133

(0, 0), which is just vocab. Know it (which you do now) and you get it correct!

$$\frac{y-y}{x-x} = \frac{-3-0}{2-0} = \frac{-3}{2}$$

Notice how $\frac{-3}{2}$ is not a choice. Don't be thrown. Be confident, unshakeable! After you finish this book, you will always know what to do; don't let the question intimidate you. So, which choice matches our $\frac{-3}{2}$? Just enter it in your calculator, remember that $\frac{-3}{2}$ means "-3 divided by 2," and you get -1.5. Bingo!

3. **C** Use two points to count the $\frac{rise}{run}$, the change in y over the change in x.

4. **C** Remember that pictures on the SAT are drawn exactly to scale (we'll talk more about this excellent strategy in Skill 21). So just use the picture to determine the values of (a, b); it looks like $(4, 4)$. The question just asks for $\frac{b}{a}$, so the answer is choice C, since $\frac{4}{4} = 1$.

5. **B** To get the slope of MN, we must know the coordinates for M and for N. Since these points are centers of the circles, they are halfway between the endpoints of each diameter shown. So M equals $(2, 1)$ and N equals $(7, 3)$. Now we plug these into the slope formula.

$$\frac{1-3}{2-7} = \frac{-2}{-5} = \frac{2}{5}$$

Skill 12 (page 33)

Slaloming Slope II

1. **A** Plug the two points into the slope equation.

$$\frac{0-3}{-1-2} = \frac{-3}{-3} = 1$$ Since we want the line to be perpendicular, take the negative reciprocal, -1.

2. **E** Parallel lines have equal slopes. The slope of line $y = -2x - 3$ is -2 (which we will review in Skill 30), so the slope of the two points given is $\frac{-3-p}{4-2} = -2$ "Use the Answers" or cross-multiply (see Skill 20) to solve for p. $p = -7$.

3. **B** The origin means $(0, 0)$. Plug the two points into the slope equation.

$$\frac{-3-0}{2-0} = -\frac{3}{2}$$

Since we want the slope of a line perpendicular, we take the negative reciprocal, which is $\frac{2}{3}$.

4. **D** This question is quite difficult for most students. But with our strategies it's very easy. We know that two lines that are reflections of each other have slopes with opposite signs, so instead of 2/3, line n has a slope of $-2/3$.

5. **C** Use the slope formula to solve for b. Then use the value of b in the slope formula for the second pair of points, and solve for m. Because the lines are parallel, the second pair also has a slope equal to 1.

Skill 13 (page 35)

Using Tables, Bar Graphs, and Pie Graphs

1. **C** Test each choice. Choice I is correct since i represents the total of $c + f$, which is the total of $a + b + d + e$. That is why II is also correct. Choice III, however, is false since $g + c$ does not equal i.

2. **275** Since Sra. Moran and Mrs. Nicholas received the most votes, they must represent the 30% and 25% sections which are largest. These add up to 55%. Since there were 500 students surveyed, we want 55% of 500 which means $0.55 \times 500 = 275$.

3. **D** Use the graph to estimate sales for each book. Then add those up and divide by 4 to get the average. Notice that the graph tells us that the numbers represent thousands of books! So the answer is choice D. Remember, the key to tables and graphs is to read the headings and legend, if there is one.

4. **A** This is an unusual graph, but one that the SAT uses quite often. If it seems difficult, work with it until it makes sense. The coordinates of each point represent the student's score on the

two tests. So we are looking for a point where the y value (test II) is bigger than the x value (test I). Even though we cannot determine exact values on the graph, point A (70, 90) clearly has the largest increase from test I to test II. Point B improves less (70, 80), and the other three choices went down from test I to test II.

Skill 14 (page 37)

The Only Function Questions on the SAT, Type I

1. **A** Simply plug -2 in for x in the equation. $f(-2) = 2(-2)^3 - 2 = -18$.

2. **D** The long way to solve this question is to plug (5) and (-5) into each equation in the answer choices to see which one makes $f(5) < f(-5)$. This absolutely works and is worth the time since it will earn you points. There is also a faster way. In every other answer choice, 5 plugged in for x will clearly give the same or higher value than when -5 is plugged in. However, choice D, $f(x) = 2 - x^3$, is the only one where a positive number yields a lower result than a negative: $2 - 5^3 < 2 - (-5)^3 \Rightarrow -123 < 127$.

3. **D** This is a very common SAT question. Just choose an (x, y) point from the table and see which equation works. Choice D is correct since $11 = 3(2)^2 - 1$. Try all equations, in case several work. Then you would just choose a second point to find the one answer choice that works for both points.

4. **E** This is a very typical SAT question, appearing on nearly every SAT. If you got this question wrong and you spend the time to master it, you will gain points! In this question, you are given values for the number of cars, which is x, and for pints of soap, which is $g(x)$. $g(x) = 140$ and $x = 3$. Simply plug these values in for x and $g(x)$, and use basic algebra to solve for k. If this is confusing, redo this question over and over until you can teach it to a friend. Then do that! This is a great party question. Next time

you go to a party, bring this one, people love it. OK, I'm kidding.

$$g(x) = 5x - (4x + k)$$
$$3 = 5(140) - (4(140) + k)$$
$$3 = 700 - 560 - k$$
$$3 = 140 - k$$
$$-137 = -k$$
$$137 = k$$

5. **D** Plug 6 into the m function, plug 3 into the h function, and subtract the results.

6. **E** $f(3)$ means "plug 3 in for x" and get y. Usually we use an equation to answer this, but in this question we use the graph shown. We simply locate $x = 3$ on the graph and see what the y value is at that point. $y = -2$. Then the question asks for $f(-2)$, so we look on the graph once again, but this time we plug -2 in for x. The best answer is $y = -\frac{11}{3}$.

Skill 15 (page 39)

The Only Function Questions on the SAT, Type II

1. **C** This question asks you if $f(m)$ equals -3, what is m? To solve, simply plug m in for x and -3 for the result: $-3 = 2(m)^2 - 3$. Then use algebra to solve for m, or "Use the Answers."

2. **D** Simply plug a in for x and -39 in for $f(x)$. Then solve for a. This question has one additional part. Once you know the value of the variable a, you have to plug that value in for the a in $4 - 2a$ to get $4 - 2(-2) = 4 + 4 = 8$.

3. **B** This question asks when $y = 2$ on the graph, what is the value of x ? Look on the graph at the y values. There are two points on the graph where $y = 2$. These two points occur at $x = 4$ or $x = -4$. Since $x = 4$ is not a choice, choice B is the answer.

4. **A** Plug $(p - 1)$ in for n in the $m(n)$ function. $m(p - 1) = (p - 1)^2 + (p - 1) = p^2 - 2p + 1 + p - 1 = p^2 - p$ which matches choice A: $h(p) = p^2 - p$.

5. **38** People hate this question, but once you know the trick, it's easy! For $3h(v) = 54$, just

use basic algebra and divide both sides by 3 to get $h(v)$ alone; $h(v) = 18$. Now, this is just a type II question—you are given the result and you must find v. Plug v in for x and 18 in for $h(x)$: $v - 2 = 18$, so $v = 20$. Cake! Last step: the question did not ask for v, that might have made it "medium" difficulty. It asks for one more step. Once you know the value of v, the question asks for $h(2v)$. Easy, $h(2v) = h(2\cdot20) = h(40) = 40 - 2 = 38$. I know, this question asks a lot; it's definitely a "hard," but if you stay focused and use these tools, you can get it.

6. ⓪ $g(3m) = 3g(m)$ means $(3m)^2 - 3 = 3(m^2 - 3)$. Use algebra to solve for m.

$$(3m)^2 - 3 = 3(m^2 - 3)$$
$$9m^2 - 3 = 3m^2 - 9$$
$$6m^2 = -6$$
$$m^2 = -1$$

Since m is a real number, m^2 cannot equal -1, so there are zero solutions.

Skill 16 (page 41)

Make It Real

1. Ⓒ This question intimidates some students; it seems too theoretical. But "Make It Real" makes it so easy. Just choose a real number for p (remember that the question says that the number that you choose has to be even). Let's say $p = 4$. Then try $p = 4$ in all the answer choices to see which one does what the question asks, which one gives us an even number. The answer is choice C since $2(4) - 2 = 2$.

2. Ⓑ "Make It Real." Let's say $x = 5$ and $n = 1$. Now it's easy, "5 days ago Striped was born and she is now 1 day older than Yellow." So Striped is 5 days old and 1 day older than Yellow, who must therefore be 4 days old. When we plug our numbers, $x = 5$ and $n = 1$, into each answer choice, the one that gives 4 is correct. Choice B is correct, $5 - 1 = 4$.

3. Ⓔ Easy, choose a number for p, let's say $p = -3$ (Notice the question states that p must

be negative. Underline that vocab word!) Now use your calculator to solve $(5 \times 10^{-3}) + (1 \times 10^{-3}) = 0.006$. Remember to use the order of operations. Whichever choice yields 0.006 is correct. Choice E is correct, $6(10)^{-3} = 0.006$.

4. Ⓓ Let's say $q = 5$. Now just follow the directions. $5 \times 7 = 35$. $35 + 7 = 42$. $42/7 = 6$. When $q = 5$, the answer is 6. So plug 5 in for q in the answer choices; whichever one equals 6 is correct. Choice D is correct, $5 + 1 = 6$.

5. Ⓔ We are into the "hards" now. But "Make It Real" will knock these down a notch to mediums or even easies. Still, since they are "hards," we may have to try several different numbers to find the one right answer. In this question, m can be any number between -2 and 5, and n can be any number between -1 and 2. Let's choose a few possibilities and see which choice always works.

If $m = -2$ and $n = -1$, $mn = 2$.
If $m = 5$ and $n = 2$, $mn = 10$, so since it can be as high as 10, choices A and B can be eliminated.
If $m = -2$ and $n = 2$, $mn = -2$.
If $m = 5$ and $n = -2$, $mn = -5$.

So, choice E is the only answer that includes all the possibilities. Notice that the best way to determine all the possibilities is to use the most extreme values for each interval and multiply them.

6. Ⓒ So easy with "Make It Real!" Let's say $n = -0.5$. Then $n^2 = 0.25$ and $n^3 = -0.125$. n^2 is the greatest since it is the only positive number, and n is the least, so C is correct.

7. Ⓐ Let's say $a = 3$ and $v = 4$. Then

$$m = \frac{3a^2}{v} = \frac{3(3)^2}{4} = \frac{3(9)}{4} = \frac{27}{4} = 6.75.$$

If a and v are doubled, then $a = 6$ and $b = 8$ and

$$m = \frac{3a^2}{v} = \frac{3(6)^2}{8} = \frac{3(36)}{8} = \frac{108}{8} = 13.5$$

Since 13.5 is double 6.75, the answer is choice A.

Skill 17 (page 43)

Perimeter, Area, Volume

1. **Ⓐ** The perimeter of the rectangle is $7 + 7 + 3 + 3 = 20$. Since the square has four equal sides and its perimeter is also 20, each side must be $20 \div 4 = 5$.

2. **Ⓑ** Since the radius of circle B is half the diameter of circle A, it must be 5. Therefore, the area of circle B is $a = \pi r^2 = \pi(5^2) = 25\pi$.

3. **Ⓒ** The surface area equals the addition of the faces. There are three square faces (area = m) and two triangular faces (area = n), so the total surface area = $3m + 2n$.

4. **Ⓒ** Since volume = length × width × height, just determine the volume for each part of the block. The smaller part = $5 \times 1 \times 1 = 5$, and the larger part = $5 \times 3 \times 1 = 15$. So the volume of the whole block = $5 + 15 = 20$.

Skill 18 (page 45)

Donuts

1. **Ⓒ** If the perimeter of square $BCDF$ is 24, each side is 6 and the area is 36. The area of $ACEG$ is $A = (l)(w) = (18)(10) = 180$. So the area of the shaded region is $180 - 36 = 144$.

2. **Ⓐ** The area of the larger circle is $A = \pi r^2 = \pi(8)^2 = 64\pi$. The radius of the smaller circle is half the radius of the larger circle. So the area of the smaller circle is $A = \pi r^2 = \pi(4)^2 = 16\pi$. The area of the unshaded region is $64\pi - 16\pi = 48\pi$.

3. **39** Fun question. Remember that the area of a shaded region equals area of big guy minus area of donut hole. The area of the whole rectangle is $6 \times 9 = 54$, and the area of the unshaded triangle is (this is the cool part) $a = 0.5bh = 0.5(5)(6) = 15$. It looks like the height wasn't given, but it is; it's 6, it's as tall as the rectangle. So the shaded region = $54 - 15 = 39$.

4. **9** Since the triangles are similar, their sides are proportional (more on this in Skill 25).

   Therefore, $\dfrac{AD}{ED} = \dfrac{BD}{CD}$ and $\dfrac{4}{2} = \dfrac{6}{CD}$,

so $CD = 3$. (How would you know to set this up? You'll see that Mantra 25 says, "Similar triangles have sides that are proportional," so when the SAT says "similar," that's what they want you to set up. That's how to think like a math genius!) The area of the larger triangle is 0.5(base)(height) = 0.5(4)(6) = 12, and the area of the smaller triangle is 0.5(base)(height) = 0.5(2)(3) = 3. So the area of the shaded region is $12 - 3 = 9$.

Skill 19 (page 47)

Baking Granola Bars . . . Ratios

1. **Ⓑ** When the SAT says the ratio of carrots to potatoes is 2 to 7, that can be the actual numbers of carrots and potatoes or a reduced version of the actual numbers. For example, instead of 2 : 7 it could be 4 : 14 or 6 : 21 or any multiple of 2 : 7. Therefore, the top number, which represents carrots, must be a multiple of 2.

2. **Ⓒ** When the SAT says that 2 out of 5 are pears, that can be the actual numbers of pears or a reduced version of the actual numbers. Since 2 out of 5 are pears, 3 out of 5 are apples, and the actual number of apples must be a multiple of 3.

3. $\dfrac{2}{3}$ or 0.666 or 0.667. "Fraction" is a synonym for "ratio"—they mean the same thing. So we just want the ratio of questions that are not true/false to total questions. Out of 60 questions, 20 were true/false, so 40 were not true/false questions. Thus, the ratio (aka fraction) of not true/false to total is 40 : 60 or $\dfrac{2}{3}$.

4. **Ⓓ** The measures of the angles must add up to 180°. Obviously 1 : 3 : 5 does not add up to 180, so multiply all three by the same number until we get 180. $1 : 3 : 5 \Rightarrow 2 : 6 : 10 \Rightarrow 10 : 30 : 50 \Rightarrow 20 : 60 : 100$. That adds up to 180, so the smallest angle is 20°.

5. **Ⓑ** This question uses the same process as Question 4 with one extra step. Once you

137

know the angles, just subtract the smallest from the largest: $100 - 20 = 80$. Some students get this wrong because they do not finish it; they see the choices 20 or 100 and choose one. This is a great careless error to practice avoiding (Skill 42).

6. **4.8** You are given the ratio of pretzels to corn chips but are asked for the ratio of pretzels to total mixture. So switch it to pretzels to total. There are 3 ounces of pretzels per 7 ounces of corn chips, so there are 10 ounces total $(3 + 7 = 10)$. The ratio of pretzels to total is 3 to 10. Thus, $\frac{3}{10} = \frac{p}{16}$
When you see a proportion, cross-multiply. $p = 4.8$.

Skill 20 (page 49)

Proportions and Cross-Multiplying

1. **C** Just set up the proportion. $\frac{15}{50} = \frac{x}{1}$.
Remember to set it up so that flour is on top in both ratios. If does not actually matter if it's on top or bottom, just that it is in the same spot in both. Then cross-multiply and solve for x.
$(15)(1) = (50)(x)$ divide both sides by 50
$x = 0.3$

2. **A** Without our cross-multiplying technology this question could be quite vexing. But cross-multiply and it's easy. Pretty much anytime you see a proportion, cross-multiply. $mn = 60$.

3. **E** Cross-multiply. $mn = 36m$. To solve for n, divide both sides by $m \cdot n = 36$.

4. **D** Let's convert $\frac{1}{4}$ into a decimal (just divide 1 by 4, which equals 0.25) and set up the proportion.
$\frac{0.25}{4} = \frac{1.5}{x}$
Cross-multiply and simply solve for x.
$6 = 0.25x$, so $x = 24$.

5. **D** Without cross-multiplying, this question would be difficult. However, just cross-multiply each answer choice. All are equal $(mp = on)$, except choice D $(mn = op)$.

Skill 21 (page 51)

Use the Diagram

1. **B** First, draw point A into the diagram; always draw any info from the question into the diagram. Since $NA = AO$, point A is in the middle (the midpoint) of NO. Using the diagram, you can then see that if MO equals 12, MA must be less, but not 6, which would be only half of 12. So the only answer that can work is 9.

2. **E** I will show you the exact geometry for a question like this in Skill 23, but for now, here's the "Use the Diagram" shortcut. First, draw M into the diagram. Then just estimate its length and translate each of the answers into decimals and choose the one closest to your estimate.

3. **A** Easy. The radius of the large circle is 6, so the diameter is 12. Use this to estimate the perimeter of the weirdly shaped unshaded region. Then translate each answer from π to decimals and see which one is closest to your estimate. This strategy works so well because usually the answer choices are far enough apart that our estimate works.

4. **A** Draw JM and based on LK, estimate its length. If we say $LK = 1$, then JM seems to be approximately 1.8. So the ratio is $1/1.8 = 0.555$. Translate the answer choices to decimals and choice A is closest.

Skill 22 (page 53)

Art Class

1. **D** Draw a diagram. Since N is between M and O, LN must be longer than 12 and shorter than 24. Only choice D is a possibility.

2. **3 or 7** Without a sketch, this is tough; with a diagram, it's easy. b can be 3 or 7.

3. **C** When you redraw to scale, often the answer becomes obvious. With all sides equal and $\angle AGE = 90°$, AE is slightly longer than CE. So the ratio of AE to CE = approximately 1.5 to 1. Translate the answers to decimals, and only choice C is close to 1.5. You could also use special right triangles (Skill 24).

4. **A** Draw a diagram. The diagram shows that the segment must be less than 2, perhaps 1.5. Convert the answers to decimals and only choices A and B are possible. The answer is choices A because the segment forms a special right triangle with sides 1, 1, and $\sqrt{2}$ (another preview of Skill 24).

5. **E** Redraw to scale; KL should be drawn a little shorter to make it 4 (a third of LN). Then using lengths that we are given as a key, we estimate JM, which is clearly a little more than 12. So only choices D and E are possible, and choice E is likely. This is an awesome strategy; we eliminated three choices on a "hard" question. The correct answer is choice E. To get an exact answer, we need, once again, special right triangles. Let's hear it for Skill 24, on the way!

Skill 23 (page 55)

The 6-Minute Abs of Geometry: Length of a Side I

1. **C** Anytime you see a right triangle on the SAT, try $a^2 + b^2 = c^2$. Also, for any question with a diagram, mark info from the question into the diagram. Here m and n are the short sides, and o is the longest (also called the hypotenuse), so $5^2 + 12^2 = o^2$, so $169 = o^2$ and $o = 13$.

2. **15** Here 8 and p are the short sides (the longest side is always opposite the right angle). So

$$8^2 + p^2 = 17^2$$
$$64 + p^2 = 289$$
$$p^2 = 225$$
$$p = 15$$

3. **B** When a picture is described but not shown, draw a diagram. This helps you visualize and organize the info and shows you what to do next. The question does not state whether 10 is another short side like 4 or if it is the longest side. But we can "Use the Answers." Simply try each answer choice along with 10 and 4 in $a^2 + b^2 = c^2$, always using the biggest number for c. To make that easier, convert all the choices to decimals. Choice A is not correct since $4^2 + (2\sqrt{19})^2 \neq 10^2$. Choice B is correct since $4^2 + (2\sqrt{21})^2 = 10^2$.

4. **15** When a picture is described, but not shown, draw a diagram. This helps you visualize and organize the info and shows you what to do next. Once we see the diagram, piece of cake. We know the hypotenuse is 13, and we see that the length of one side is 5, so $5^2 + b^2 = 13^2$. Use algebra to get $b = 12$. But now don't forget to finish. The length of b is 12, so $m = 12 + 3 = 15$.

5. **A** If the longest side is x and the lengths of the sides are consecutive integers, then the shorter sides can be called $(x - 1)$ and $(x - 2)$. Now, we just plug these into $a^2 + b^2 = c^2$ to get $(x - 2)^2 + (x - 1)^2 = x^2$.

Skill 24 (page 57)

The 6-Minute Abs of Geometry: Length of a Side II

1. **A** When a picture is described but not shown, draw a diagram. This helps you visualize and organize the info and shows you what to do next. The question does not state whether 8 is another short side like 4 or if it is the longest side. But we can "Use the Answers." Simply try each answer choice in $a^2 + b^2 = c^2$, always using the biggest number for c. Choice I is not correct since $4^2 + 4^2 \neq 8^2$, choice II is correct since $4^2 + 4\sqrt{3}^2 = 8^2$, and choice III is not correct since $4^2 + 2^2 \neq 8^2$.

2. **C** As soon as you see a right triangle with a 60° angle, use the special right triangle 30, 60, 90. The hypotenuse is 12, so the smallest leg

must be 6. A triangle congruent to the one shown will also have a shortest leg of 6, since they are congruent.

3. **B** An isosceles right triangle is a right triangle where two sides are the same length. When two sides are equal (great review from Skill 6), their two opposite angles are also equal. Therefore, we have a 90, 45, 45 triangle. Since the two equal sides add up to 6, each is 3, and the longest side is $3\sqrt{2}$

4. **E** In Skill 22, we redrew the diagram to scale and estimated the answer. With special right triangles we can get the exact answer. As soon as you see a right triangle with a 30° angle, use the special right triangle 30, 60, 90. We are given the longest side $LN = 10$, so the side opposite the 30° angle is 5 and LM is $5\sqrt{3}$. Similarly, since $KL = 6$, $KJ = 3$ and $JL = 3\sqrt{3}$ Thus, $JM = 5\sqrt{3} + 3\sqrt{3} = 8\sqrt{3}$.

Skill 25 (page 59)

The 6-Minute Abs of Geometry: Length of a Side III

1. **B** Triangle ABC is isosceles, so $AB = BC$. Similar triangles have proportional sides, so

$$\frac{BC}{NO} = \frac{AC}{MO} \Rightarrow \frac{4}{6} = \frac{3}{MO}$$

When you see a proportion, cross-multiply, so $4MO = 18$, and $MO = 4.5$.

2. **B** When a picture is described but not shown, draw it. Fill in the sides of special right triangle PQR: 3, $3\sqrt{3}$, 6. The sides of similar triangle MNO must be proportional to the sides of PQR, so the sides of MNO must be multiples of 3, $3\sqrt{3}$, 6. Choice B is correct since 6, $6\sqrt{3}$, $12 = 2(3, 3\sqrt{3}, 6)$.

3. **D** When you see a right triangle, try $a^2 + b^2 = c^2$. Based on the diagram, $3^2 + b^2 = 5^2$, so $b = 4$. Then when a picture is described but not shown, draw it. Draw PRQ and fill in the sides of both triangles. Since the triangles are similar, their sides are proportional. The ratio of the small side of one triangle to the small

side of the other is given as 2 or 2 : 1, so the lengths of all the sides of the pictured triangle are twice those of triangle PRQ. Thus, the perimeter, which is 12, of the triangle shown must be twice the perimeter of PRQ, which is therefore 6.

4. **D** Similar triangles have proportional sides. We are told that the ratio between the sides is 3 : 5. Therefore, the ratio of the smallest sides is $\frac{x}{4} = \frac{3}{5}$.

Skill 26 (page 63)

"Is" Means Equals . . . Translation

1. **C** This is direct translation. Product means multiply and sum means add, so $(b)(2) = b + \frac{2}{3}$ or $2b = b + \frac{2}{3}$

2. **B** Each foot has 12 inches, so f feet has $12f$ inches, and c inches is just c inches, so there is a total of $12f + c$.

3. **D** Translate and solve. $p + 6 = 5p$, so $p = 1.5$. Then remember that the question did not ask for p—it asked for $8p$, so simply multiply $8(1.5) = 12$. This is a great careless error to learn to avoid; many students lose points by forgetting to finish the question. This is normal, since your math teacher always asks for p, not $8p$. But, now you know to expect this on the SAT, and you won't lose points.

4. $\frac{2}{3}$, 0.666, or 0.667. Translate: $2x + 3y = 1.20(5y)$. Normally in school you solve for x or y. This question asks you to solve for $\frac{y}{x}$. No biggie, just manipulate the equation to get $\frac{y}{x}$ on one side.

$$2x + 3y = 1.20(5y)$$
$$2x + 3y = 6y$$
$$2x = 3y$$
$$\frac{2}{3} = \frac{y}{x}$$

5. **E** Translate and solve for m. $(m + 11)^2 = (m + 1)^2 (9)$. To simplify, take the square root of both sides to eliminate the squares to get

$m + 11 = (m + 1)(3)$

$m + 11 = 3m + 3$

$8 = 2m$

$4 = m$

you could also "Use the Answers."

Skill 27 (page 65)

Just Do It! . . . Springboard

1. **D** Classic springboard. If you see a fraction that can be reduced, do it. So $\frac{3}{18} = \frac{1}{6} = \frac{a}{k}$, so k could equal 6.

2. **D** If you see something that can be multiplied, do it. $p(p + 2) = p^2 + 2p$, so $m = p^2 + 2p$. To find $m - 3$, we just subtract 3 from both sides to get $m - 3 = p^2 + 2p - 3$.

3. **12** If you see $x^2 - y^2$, factor it, so $(x - y)(x + y) = 108$, and we are told that $(x + y) = 9$, so $9(x - y) = 108$, and $(x - y) = 12$.

4. **B** If something can be FOILed, do it. $(x + n)(x + 1) = x^2 + 1x + nx + n$. Since that also equals $x^2 + mx + 5$, we know that $n = 5$, and therefore $m = 1 + 5 = 6$.

5. **C** If you see something that can be simplified, do it.

$12\sqrt{12} = 12\sqrt{4 \cdot 3} = 12 \cdot 2\sqrt{3} = 24\sqrt{3}$

So $p = 24$ and $q = 3$ and $\frac{p}{q} = 8$.

6. **B** If something can be FOILed, do it. $(x - 3y)^2 = (x - 3y)(x - 3y) = x^2 - 6xy + 9y^2$. Since $xy = 11$, $x^2 = 5$, and $y^2 = 7$, we have all the parts and $x^2 - 6xy + 9y^2 = 5 - 6(11) + 9(7) = 2$.

Skill 28 (page 67)

Beyond Your Dear Aunt Sally:
The Laws of Exponents I

1. **A** When you multiply variables, like x, you add the exponents, so $(x^2)(2x^3) = 2x^5$.

2. **C** $(3m^4)(2b^4) = 6m^4b^4 = 6(mb)^4$. Notice that this time I did not add the exponents because

m and b are different letters, and we only add when the letters are the same.

3. **E** Great "Use the Answers" review. Since there are variables in the question and numbers in the answer choices, we can try the answers. The question asks for the greatest value of b, so we'll start with the biggest choice, 5. Plugging 5 in for b in the question, we get $2^a \cdot 2^5 = 64$. $2^5 = 32$, so $2^a \cdot 32 = 64$. Divide both sides by 32 to get $2^a = 2$, which could work if $a = 1$. Thus, 5 works for b and is the largest choice.

4. **D** Great vocab review; underline "different positive integers." Often, noticing and remembering to apply these words is the key to the question. Also great "Use the Answers" review. Since there are variables in the question and numbers in the answer choices, we can try the answers. The question asks for the greatest value of p, so we'll start with the biggest choice, 5. Since we want p to be as big as possible, we'll make m and n as low as possible, 1 and 2, since they need to be "**different** positive integers." Plug 5 in for p in the question; we get $2^1 \cdot 2^2 \cdot 2^5 \neq 128$. Trying $p = 4$, we get $2^1 \cdot 2^2 \cdot 2^4 = 128$, which works.

5. **A** For $p^m \cdot p^6 = p^{12}$, we add the exponents, so $m = 6$. For $(p^3)^n = p^{21}$, we multiply the exponents, so $n = 7$. So $n - m = 1$.

6. **A** "What is the value of b in terms of a?" means solve for b, get b alone. To get b alone and eliminate the exponent, we take the eighth root of each side ($\sqrt[8]{}$), since $\sqrt[8]{b}$ is the opposite of b^8. So, taking the $\sqrt[8]{}$ of both sides, we get $\sqrt[8]{a^4} = a^{1/2} = b$. We will deal with this more in Skill 29.

Skill 29 (page 69)

Far Beyond Your Dear Aunt Sally:
The Laws of Exponents II

1. **C** $2x^2$ and $2x^3$ are not like terms and do not combine. To combine, the variable (x) **and** the exponents would have to match.

2. **B** Since both terms have an x^2, they are like terms. To add them, we add their coefficients. "Coefficient" is the fancy vocab term for the number in front of the variable. So $4x^2 + 5x^2 = 9x^2$.

3. **A** To multiply $3m^{-2}$ by $2m^{-5}$, we add the exponents, so $(3m^{-2})(2m^{-5}) = 6m^{-7} = \dfrac{6}{m^7}$

4. **D** Great question $3^{n/p}$ means $\sqrt[p]{3^n}$. So $\sqrt[p]{3^n} = \sqrt{27}$. And $3^n = 27$, so $n = 3$ and $p = 2$. So $(n)(p) = (3)(2) = 6$.

5. **E** For $p^m \cdot p^{-4} = p^5$, we add the exponents, so $m = 9$. For $(p^{-2})^n = p^{20}$, we multiply the exponents, so $n = -10$. So $n - m = -10 - 9 = -19$.

6. **C** Somehow, we need to get 243^{-1}, meaning we need to get $\dfrac{1}{243}$ using 3s. This should stir you to play with your calculator and arrive at $3^5 = 243$ and $3^{-5} = \dfrac{1}{243}$. So $m + n + p = -5$. Since they all must be negative numbers, they can be $-1, -2, -2$, or $-1, -1 - 3$. So $nmp = -4$ or -3.

Skill 30 (page 71)

Your Algebra Teacher Never Said "$y = ax + b$"

1. **E** 25 people are offended by each joke, so that number goes next to x. 50 people are offended right off the bat, and this number does not change with the number of outrageous jokes in the movie, so that number goes alone. $y = 25x + 50$.

2. **-1** If you are given a point and an equation, plug in the point and solve for the unknown:
$y = -2x + 3$
$g = -2(2) + 3$
$g = -1$

3. **E** If you are give a point and an equation, plug in the point and solve for the unknown.

So plug $(2,1)$ into $y = mx - 2$ to get $m = \dfrac{3}{2}$. Since line k is perpendicular to line j, its slope must be $-\dfrac{2}{3}$ Thus, $y = -\dfrac{2}{3}x + b$. Again, plug in $(2,1)$ to get $y = -\dfrac{2}{3}x + \dfrac{7}{3}$

4. **B** Great question; most SATs have one like this. Alex knew that $b = 4$, so the y intercept is 4, and that a is positive, so the graph rises from left to right. (Review slope in Skill 11 if needed. If you slacked during the slope chapter and did not do the drills, e-mail me and I'll send a motivational speech your way.) Choice B is the only choice that satisfies both requirements of y intercept of 4 and positive slope.

Skill 31 (page 73)

Arrangements I

1. **6** Draw a blank for each option. Then write in the number of possibilities that can fill each option. There are 2 slogan options and 3 size options, so $\underline{2} \times \underline{3} = 6$. Notice that this question is simple enough to do without the strategy, you could just picture shirts in piles, like at Old Navy, with two different slogans available in S, M, and L, making 6 piles.

2. **D** Draw a blank for each role that needs to be filled by an actor. Then write in the number of actors who can fill the role. Remember that each actor can play only one role, so once someone is assigned, that actor can't be used again. Then multiply.
$\underline{5} \times \underline{4} \times \underline{3} \times \underline{2} \times \underline{1} = 120$

3. **D** Draw a blank for each spot at the burrito bar. Then write in the number of possibilities that can fill each slot. There are 3 options for meat, 3 options for vegetables, and 4 options for salsas, so
$\underline{3} \times \underline{3} \times \underline{4} = 36$

4. **E** Draw a blank for each digit of the four-digit number. Fill in the number of possible digits that can go in each blank. No digit can be used more than once. So, $\underline{4} \times \underline{3} \times \underline{2} \times \underline{1} = 24$.

5. **64** Draw a blank for each digit of the three-digit number. Fill in the number of possible digits that can go in each blank. There are 4 prime numbers that can fill each blank: 2, 3, 5, and 7. Remember that 1 is not prime, but 2 is. Notice that the question does not say that a digit can be used only once. So, $\underline{4} \times \underline{4} \times \underline{4} = 64$.

6. **60** Draw a blank for each spot on the banner. Fill in the number of possible symbols that can go in each spot. Notice that the three symbols must be different. So, $\underline{5} \times \underline{4} \times \underline{3} = 60$.

Skill 32 (page 75)

Arrangements II

1. **15** Draw a blank for each member of the doubles team. Write in the number of possible girls who can fill each slot; remember that once someone is assigned a position, she cannot also play another position. Then multiply. This question has one extra step, since this is a team of two. It does not matter if it's Jenny and Jill or Jill and Jenny; we divide our answer by 2 since we will have double-counted each duo.

$\underline{6} \times \underline{5} = 30 \div 2 = 15$

2. **B** Draw a blank for each slot of the three-digit number. Fill in the restricted slots first; since the number must be greater than 200, the first digit cannot be 1 and is restricted to 2 possibilities, the digits 2 or 3. Then fill in the other, nonrestricted slots with the number of possible digits that can fill each blank, and multiply.

$\underline{2} \times \underline{2} \times \underline{1} = 4$

3. **C** Draw a blank for each slot of the four-digit number. Write the number of possible digits that can fill each blank, filling choice in restricted slots first. The first digit has 9 possibilities, 1–9. It cannot be 0 since that would make the number a three-digit, not a

four-digit, number. The next two slots can be 10 possibilities, 0–9. And, the last digit can be 5 possibilities that would make the four-digit number even, 0, 2, 4, 6, 8. Then multiply.

$\underline{9} \times \underline{10} \times \underline{10} \times \underline{5} = 4500$

4. **360** Draw a blank for each slot of the three-digit number. Write the number of possible digits that can fill each blank, filling in restricted spots first. The units digit must be prime, so there are four possibilities (2, 3, 5, 7). The hundreds digit can have nine possibilities (1 through 9), and the tens digit has 10 possibilities (0 through 10). So $\underline{9} \times \underline{10} \times \underline{4} = 360$.

5. **48** Draw a blank for each of the five symbols that we will place. Fill in the restricted slots first; since the γ is never in the middle three spots, fill in these first. Once a symbol is placed, we can't use it again, so the middle slots have 4, 3, and 2 possibilities. Then either end slot can include the γ, so there are 2 and 1 possibilities. Fill in the slots and multiply.

$\underline{2} \times \underline{4} \times \underline{3} \times \underline{2} \times \underline{1} = 48$

6. **C** Draw a blank for each position to be filled. Then fill in the restricted slots first; there are only 3 players able to pitch or catch. Once a pitcher is chosen, 2 are left to possibly catch. Once the pitcher and catcher are chosen, there are 4 kids still available for the remaining positions. Fill in these slots and multiply.

$\underset{\text{Pitcher}}{\underline{3}} \times \underset{\text{Catcher}}{\underline{2}} \times \underset{\text{Other}}{\underline{4}} \times \underset{\text{Other}}{\underline{3}} \times \underset{\text{Other}}{\underline{2}} = 144$

Skill 33 (page 77)

What You Really Want . . . Probability

1. **B** Probability $= \frac{\text{want}}{\text{total}}$, so the probability of selecting a blue marble is $\frac{4}{12}$. This question requires that we reduce the $\frac{4}{12}$ to $\frac{1}{3}$. No problem, stop looking at me like that, reducing is easy, just divide the top and bottom of the fraction by the same number. Or, if you really don't like reducing, just use your calculator. Divide 4 by

12 to get 0.333. Then divide each answer choice (top by the bottom) to get decimals and see which one matches 0.333. Nice.

2. $\frac{1}{3} = 0.333$. Great vocab review! Remember that 1 is not a prime number. So since Probability $= \frac{\text{want}}{\text{total}}$, the probability of randomly selecting a prime number from the set is $\frac{2}{6} = \frac{1}{3} = 0.33$. When you take the SAT, remember that if you have a long decimal number, you have to use enough digits to fill in the student-produced response grid, so 0.33 would be marked wrong and we need 0.333!

3. **D** Since the probability of selecting a carrot is 1 out of 4, there are 4 vegetables in the basket or a multiple of 4 since $\frac{1}{4}$ could be a reduced version of the actual number. Thus, only choice D works since 8 is the only multiple of 4 in the choices.

4. **C** Since Probability $= \frac{\text{want}}{\text{total}}$ and the probability of obscenities is $\frac{7}{12}$, there are 7 scenes with obscenities for every 12 scenes of the movie. Thus, there are 5 scenes of nonobscenities, $12 - 7 = 5$. $n = 5$ and $c = 7$, so $\frac{n}{c} = \frac{5}{7}$.

5. $\frac{1}{4}$. Since the question states that either team has an equal chance of winning, the probability of Northampton winning each game is 1 out of 2, or $\frac{1}{2}$. The probability of winning both games is $\frac{1}{2} \times \frac{1}{2} = \frac{1}{4}$.

Skill 34 (page 79)
Median and Mode

1. **28** Simply draw blanks for the 7 numbers and place 31 in the middle blank. Then fill in the consecutive numbers above and below 31.

"Consecutive" means numbers in a row, for example, 28, 29, 30, 31, 32, 33, 34. So the smallest number is 28.

2. **A** First add Don's score to the table—there are now 2 bowlers who scored a 140. The mode is the number in the list that occurs most often. According to the table there are 4 bowlers who scored 130, so 130 is the mode. Then to find the median, rewrite the data as a list in order. The middle number is 135, and the median minus the mode is $135 - 130 = 5$.

3. **A** Simply plug each answer in for the variable. If $m = 2$, then the list is 2, 5, 2 and $2m - 2$, which equals 2, is the mode.

4. **D** Increasing the largest number does not affect the median. No matter how big the biggest number becomes, the middle number is still in the middle of the list. Tripling each number will completely change the numbers in the list; for example, the number 4 would become the number 12. If you were unsure for this question, you could simply make up a list of nine numbers and try the choices and see which ones change the median and which one does not.

5. **453** Rewrite the attendance numbers from the table as a list in order. Since the question states that 452 should be the median, x must be to the right of 452. The question states that no numbers are the same. So any number greater than 452 will make 452 the median, and the least x can equal is 453. Notice how simple this "hard" question is if you know the vocab and how to approach it!

Skill 35 (page 81)
$y = ax^2 + bx + c$

1. **E** On the SAT, when you are given a point (x, y) and an equation, plug the point into the equation. So plug $(0, k)$ into either equation. $k = 2(0)^2 + 3(0) + 4 = 4$. So $k = 4$.

2. **B** Just follow the same rule as in question 1. Since 0 is the only solution that works for both equations, there is one solution.

3. **E** Plug $(m, 22)$ into the first equation to solve for m. Then plug the solution into the second equation to solve for k.

$22 = 2(m)^2 + 4$
$18 = 2(m)^2$
$9 = m^2$
$+3$ or $-3 = m$

Plug $(3, 22)$ or $(-3, 22)$ into the second equation.
$22 = -(3)^2 - k$
$22 = -9 - k$
$31 = -k$
$-31 = k$

4. **E** This type of question is rated "hard," but is easy for us. Since k is negative, the U-shaped graph must open down; and since r is negative, the y intercept must be negative. Choice E is the only answer that satisfies both requirements.

Skill 36 (page 83)

"That's Illogical, Captain"

1. **D** I wear sandals when it is sunny, cloudy, or snowing, but not when it is raining. So if today I am wearing sandals, the only answer that must be true is that it is not raining. That's easy, right? The only way to get this one wrong is to rush into one of the four wrong choices or to doubt yourself, and say, "I don't get this; I'll just go with B." But if you stay relaxed and focused and confident, you can easily see why D is the correct answer.

2. **E** This question is much easier than it seems. Many students make four systems of equations and break out their TI-89 calculators to do perverse, unspeakable things involving matrices and cubic graphs. But the pig is listed in the three least weighing groups, and the mule is listed in the three highest weighing groups, so the pig must be the lightest animal and the mule the heaviest. Use that to determine that choice E is correct. Easy. Remember, with logic questions, don't get intimidated. They are easy if you relax and look for the easy answer.

3. **C** Great vocab review! Region A represents the set of all even numbers, region B represents the set of all prime numbers, and region C represents the set of odd numbers less than 50. Remember that 2 is the only even prime number, so it is the only number in region A and region B.

4. **A** The intersection of region B and region C contains all odd numbers less than 50 that are prime. Be systematic; make a list of odd prime numbers less than 50.

3, 5, 7, 11, 13, 17, 19, 23, 29, 31, 37, 41, 43, 47

5.6. **E** The Spanish Club has 23 members and the Environmental Club has 23 members, so there should be 46 members total in the two groups; but the question says that when they meet together, there are only 40 people. Thus, since $46 - 40 = 6$, and 6 members must belong to both clubs.

Skill 37 (page 85)

Hopscotch, Pigtails, and Remainders

1. **B** Your calculator tells you that 13 divided by 3 is 4.3333. That does not give us the answer. Instead we need to channel 5th grade: you haven't showered in a week, and you're sure that this next pack of baseball cards will complete your set. Now you remember, remainder is just the left over when you do long division.

```
   4 r1
3|13
   12
    1
```

2. **A** Just divide 24 by even numbers and see which answers we can cross off.

```
   1 r10      1 r8       1 r6       1 r4
14|24       16|24      18|24      20|24
   14          16         18         20
   10           8          6          4
```

So the answer is 12, since all the other answer choices can be remainders when 24 is divided by even numbers.

3. **D** This is a great review of the "Use the Answers" strategy. Just try each answer choice

to see which one does not give remainder 3 when divided by 4.

$$\begin{array}{ccccc}
\underline{1\ r3} & \underline{3\ r3} & \underline{4\ r3} & \underline{5\ r2} & \underline{6\ r3} \\
4|7 & 4|15 & 4|19 & 4|22 & 4|27 \\
\underline{4} & \underline{12} & \underline{16} & \underline{20} & \underline{24} \\
3 & 3 & 3 & 2 & 3
\end{array}$$

Each choice works EXCEPT choice D, 22, which gives a remainder of 2 not 3.

4. **A** This is a nice vocab review. Remember that "consecutive" means in a row, "positive" means greater than 0, and "integer" means no decimals. So just choose 5 consecutive positive integers and divide each by 4, and see which answer choice is correct. Remember that the correct answer might be a different starting point, but the same pattern as your numbers.

5. **E** This is a great preview of "Weird Symbol Questions" (Skill 45). This is not some symbol that you missed in algebra class. Nobody knows this symbol. The SAT is making it up and telling us what to do with it. So you just have to stay confident and roll with it. The symbol represents the remainder when the second number is divided by the first. So n divided by -18 should give a remainder of 3. Simply try each answer choice. 39 divided by -18 equals -2 with a remainder of 3.

6. **C** Another preview of "Weird Symbol Questions." The operation just represents the remainder when the first number is divided by the second number. So 24 divided by b should give a remainder of 3. What can b equal to make that work? Here's the key: if the remainder is 3, then we must multiply to get $24 - 3 = 21$. So we can divide by 7 or 21 to get remainder of 3, and there are 2 possibilities. This is a "hard" because most people who do not read this book have absolutely no idea how to do this question.

Skill 38 (page 87)

Absolute Value

1. **C** Great "Use the Answers" review! Try each answer choice in the equation. Choice C is correct, since $|6 - 18| = |-12| = 12$ and $|6 - (-6)| = |12| = 12$.

2. **D** Again, "Use the Answers." Try each answer choice in the question.

   I. $|2 + 3| = 5$ correct
   II. $|-2 + 3| \neq 5$ incorrect
   III. $|-8 + 3| = 5$ correct

   So I and III are correct, and choice D is the answer.

3. **D** Remember to underline the vocab term "negative integers" so you don't forget about it. We must consider the possible values for m and n:

   $|-7| + |-1| = 8, m = -7, n = -1$
   $|-6| + |-2| = 8, m = -6, n = -2$
   $|-5| + |-3| = 8, m = -5, n = -3$
   $|-4| + |-4| = 8, m = -4, n = -4$
   $|-3| + |-5| = 8, m = -3, n = -5$
   $|-2| + |-6| = 8, m = -2, n = -6$
   $|-1| + |-7| = 8, m = -1, n = -7$

   So try each possible pair of m and n to see which gives the least value for $m - n$.
   $-7 - (-1) = -6$ and is the least value.

4. **E** Since $x < 0$, x must equal -12 since $|4 + (-12)| = |-8| = 8$. And in the equation $|3 - y| = 5$, y equals -2 since $|3 - (-2)| = 5$. So $xy = (-12)(-2) = 24$.

5. $-1 < a < 0$. Start by just trying some numbers and see if you can get one that works. Any positive numbers yield an answer that is too large, and 0 is still too big since $|1 + 2(1)| = 1$. So try -1. $|1 + 2(-1)| = |-1| = 1$, so that doesn't work. What if $a = -0.5$? That works, so -0.5 is an answer; in fact any number between 0 and -1 works.

6. **E** Let's look at each choice. Could m equal

   I. 0   Definitely, $0 = |0|$.
   II. n Sure, $n = |n|$ could work if $n > 0$.
   III. $-n$ Sure, $-n = |n|$, if $n < 0$. Nice!

   So all three work.

Skill 39 (page 89)

Sequences I

Answer to Brian's Math Magic Trick #2: Come on, you should know that there are no elephants in Denmark! To find out how this stunning act of magic works, go to my website: www.BrianLeaf.com/Elephants.

1. **C** So easy. Just continue the sequence until you have seven terms: 3, 6, 12, 24, 48, 96, **192**.

2. $\frac{2}{3}$ or 0.666. Still easy! Just continue the sequence until you have six terms: 112, 54, 18, 6, 2, $\frac{2}{3}$

3. **19** Great vocab review! A prime integer is a number that is only divisible by 1 and itself. If the least number in the sequence is 11, the numbers must be 11, 13, 17, **19**.

4. **9** This "medium" question is easy for us. Remember to underline the vocab; we are looking for the first <u>odd</u> number in the sequence. 12, 8, 10, **9**.

5. **D** Just follow the directions closely to get the sequence: 1, 8, 22, 50, 106, 218. Then, to find the average, just add the numbers and divide by how many there are: 405/6 = 67.5.

6. **B** Draw a diagram to get the feel for this question. SAT Crasher's Rule #22: If a picture is described, draw it. The diagram allows you to see that on each roll the ball advances 6 − 1 = 5 cm. Since she is rolling it from the 15−cm mark to the 60-cm mark, the ball will travel 45 cm. So 45 cm divided by 5 cm per roll will need 9 rolls since 45/5 = 9.

Skill 40 (page 91)

Sequences II

1. **A** The sequence starts at 3 and each new term adds 3, so the 77th term will be found by starting with 3 and adding 3 for each of the next 76 terms: 3 + 76(3) = 231.

2. **A** Draw a diagram to get the feel for this question (SAT Crasher's Rule #22: If a picture

is described, draw it.) The diagram allows you to see that for each roll the ball advances 6 − 1 = 5 cm. Since she is rolling it from the 15-cm mark for 41 rolls, her final mark is 15 + 41(5) = 220.

3. **B** Continue the sequence until you see the repeating pattern:

J, A, S, O, N, J, A, S, O, N, . . .
Use the pattern to count to the 201st term, or since there are five members of the repeating pattern, divide 201 by 5 to see how many times it will repeat and then determine the remainder. 201/5 = 40 with 1 more to go. So, to get to the 201st term, Jason will write his name 40 times and then write just the first letter. The question asks for the term after he writes the 201st term, so the 202nd term is choice B.

4. **3** Continue the sequence until you see a repeating pattern:
3, 6, −6, −3. 3, 6, −6, −3, 3, . . .
You can see that the repeating pattern is 3, 6, −6, −3.
So just use the pattern to count to the 41st term, or divide 41 by 4 to see how many times you will loop the pattern. 41/4 = 10 with remainder 1. We loop the 4 terms 10 times and wind up with one more term, back at 3.

5. **E** Continue the pattern: 2x, 4x, 8x, 16x, 32x. This could have been a very tough question, but "Make It Real" makes it easy! We know that, for example, the 4th term equals 16x. So when $n = 4$, the expression should equal 16x. We try $n = 4$ in every answer choice and see which one yields 16x. Choices D and E work, so we need to try a second example as a tie breaker. When $n = 5$, the expression should equal 32x. We only need to test choices D and E, and this time, only choice E works: $2^5 x = 32x$.

6. **C** Just continue the sequence until you see a repeating pattern:
3, 0, 0, −3. 3, 0, 0, −3, 3, . . .
You can see that the repeating pattern is 3, 0, 0, −3.

Divide 167 by 4 to see how many times you will loop the pattern. $167/4 = 41$ with remainder 3. So we loop the sequence 10 times and wind up with three more terms, at 0.

Skill 41 (page 93)

Don't Even Think about It! . . . Most Common SAT Math Careless Errors I

1. **B** Nice function review! $f(-p)$ means plug $-p$ in for x. So $f(-p) = -2(-p)^3 = -2(-p^3) = 2p^3$. Careless error buster: Remember that the 2 is not inside the parentheses and does not get cubed with the p.

2. **A** Plug in $m = -1$ and simplify. $m(2x^2 - 2) = -1(2x^2 - 2) = -2x^2 + 2$. Careless error buster: Remember to distribute the negative sign!

3. **D** Plug $x = 3$ into the equation to get $y = \frac{3(a)-15}{3} = a - 5$, not $a - 15$. Careless error buster: Remember to also divide the 15 by 3.

4. **E** Plug $2p$ in for m and then FOIL $(2p + 4)^2$. You can use the algebra trick for FOILing a binomial if you know it, and if you don't, no sweat, just do it out: $(2p + 4)^2 = (2p + 4)(2p + 4) = 4p^2 + 8p + 8p + 16 = 4p^2 + 16p + 16$. Skill 42 preview: When you FOIL, remember the middle term!

5. **A** Another function review, this is a good day. This question is similar to number 3 above, but more involved. Plug $-2p$ in for x: $f(-2p) = -2p(2(-2p)^2 - 2) = -2p(2(4p^2) - 2) = -2p(8p^2 - 2) = -16p^3 + 4p$. Careless error buster: Remember to distribute the negative sign!

6. 360. Serious functions review! Plug m in for x and 27 in for the result: $27 = 3m$, so $m = 9$. Next, plug $-2m$, which we now know equals -18, into the f function: $-18(-18 - 2) = -18(-20) = +360$. Skill 42 preview: Finish the question, don't stop with $m = 9$. Remember to ask, "Did I finish the question?"

Skill 42 (page 95)

Don't Even Think about It! . . . Most Common SAT Math Careless Errors II

1. **C** Nice function review! $f(4p)$ means plug $4p$ in for x. So $f(4p) = 3(4p)^2 = 3(16p^2) = 48p^2$. Careless error buster: Remember that the 4 gets squared and that only then do you multiply by 3, not before—order of operations, my man.

2. **14** When $x = -2$, then $y = 2(-2)^2 + 4 = 12$. The question does not ask for y, but for $y + 2$, so the correct answer is $12 + 2 = 14$. This is weird since your math teacher always asks for a final answer of y, not $y + 2$. But we know the SAT does this, and we know to watch for it. Careless error buster: Remember to finish the question.

3. **E** If he rode 5 miles in 10 minutes, we could say he rode 1 mile per 2 minutes. When he later rode to his friend's house 4 miles away, it would take him (4 miles)(2 minutes/mile) = 8 minutes. Careless error buster: Remember to finish the question. 1 and 2 are offered as choices, don't finish the first calculation and go, "Sweet, there it is." Remember to finish. Ask yourself, "Did I finish the question?"

4. **D** Plug $3y$ for x into the expression $(x - 2)^2$ to get $(3y - 2)^2 = 9y^2 - 12y + 4$. Careless error buster: When you FOIL a binomial, remember the middle term.

5. **16** Plug -6 in for x: $r(-6) = \frac{-6}{3} = -2 = n$. Some people would stop here, but remember to finish the question. To find $p(-2n)$, plug -2 in for n, so $p(-2n) = p(-2(-2)) = p(4) = 2(4)(4 - 2) = 16$. Careless error buster: Remember to finish the question.

6. **3** Most kids have a tough time with this one. The key is that the distance is equal for both trips, so we set (rate)(time) equal for the way there and the way back:

(Rate)(time) = (rate)(time)
The total trip was 0.5 hour. So if we call one way t, then we can call the return trip $(0.5 - t)$.

Notice that we should use hours, not minutes, since rate is in miles per **hour**.

$10(t) = (15)(0.5 - t)$

$10t = 7.5 - 15t$

$25t = 7.5$

$t = 0.3$ hour

Now remember, the question asks how far Josh lives, NOT the time, so $D = RT$ and $D = 10$ mph$(0.3$ hour$) = 3$ miles. Careless error buster: Finish the question, don't stop with $t = 0.3$. Remember to ask, "Did I finish the question?"

Skill 43 (page 97)

Misbehaving Numbers: Weird Number Behavior

1. 0. Since $k = 0$, q must equal zero, since $2kp = 2(0)p = 0$. Anything times zero equals zero.

2. ⓔ Point N is to the left of -4, so it must be more negative than -4. Choice E is the only choice that is more negative than -4.

3. ⓒ To multiply to get zero, either $(x - 2) = 0$ or $(x + 3) = 0$. So $x = 2$ or -3.

4. ⓓ Great review of "Make It Real." Plug $m = -2$ and a value for n, say $n = 3$, into each answer choice and look for the greatest result. Choice D is correct because the even exponent cancels out the negative sign, whereas the odd exponent in choice E keeps the negative.

5. ⓑ Great "Use the Answers" review. Try each answer in the question:

   Ⓐ Nope, $-1 \neq 2(-1)$

   Ⓑ Yup, $0 = 2(0)$

   Ⓒ Nope, $1 \neq 2(1)$

   Ⓓ Nope, $2 \neq 2(2)$

   Choice B is the answer since anything times zero equals zero.

6. ⓒ "Make It Real!" Let's say $r = -2$. Plug $r = -2$ into each choice and find the greatest one. Choice C is greatest since subtracting a negative is like adding: $2 - (-2) = 4$.

7. ⓒ "Make It Real!" Let's say $x = -1.5$. Then $x = -1.5$, $x^2 = (-1.5)^2 = +2.25$, and $x^3 =$

$(-1.5)^3 = -3.375$. So the order is $x^3 < x < x^2$, since when you square a negative, it becomes positive, but when you cube a negative, it stays negative.

Skill 44 (page 99)

Mathematical Transformations

1. ⓑ The graph shown is a transformation of the parent $y = x^2$ moved down 1 unit, so $y = x^2 - 1$. You could also "Use the Answers" and graph each answer choice on your calculator to see which one matches the graph shown in the question.

2. ⓒ This is a straightforward transformation. The parent function $g(x)$ needs to be shifted 1 unit to the right. If you memorize the transformations listed in this Skill, the question is easy; a right transformation would be $y = g(x - 1)$. If you did not memorize the transformations, get to it, you silly slacker. Or, you could graph each choice on your calculator and see which one yields results that are all 1 unit to the right of the parent.

3. ⓓ This is a transformation. The graph shown in the question is $y = x^2$ moved 1 unit left. To also move it down 2 units would result in the equation $y = (x + 1)^2 - 2$. You could "Use the Answers" and use your calculator to graph each answer choice to see which one shows the graph from the question moved 2 units down.

4. ⓓ You can see that n is a transformation of m, and using a pair of points as reference, you can see that it has been moved up 1 unit and left 2 units. So, based on the equation $n(x) = m(x + h) - k$, $h = 2$ and $k = -1$. So $h - k = 2 - (-1) = 3$.

Skill 45 (page 101)

Weird Symbol Questions

1. ⓔ Just follow the directions. According to the directions, $-3 \wedge n \wedge -1$ means that $-1 > -3 > n$. Notice that this means that $n < -3$.

Try each answer. Choice E is the only choice that works.

2. **D** The directions state that ⓣ represents all of the prime factors of the number in the circle. In other words, ㉔ = 2 and 3, since these are the factors of 24 that are prime numbers. (If that is confusing, see Skills 8 and 9.) Both 2 and 3 are the prime factors of 12, 18, and 24. Choice D is correct since 2 and 3 are also the prime factors of 36.

3. **9** Just follow the directions.
$(j + 1)(j - 1)$
$(5 + 4)(5 - 4)$
$(9)(1) = 9$

4. **A** Just follow the directions.
$\lozenge m = \lozenge(m - 3)$
$m^2 + 3m = (m - 3)^2 + 3(m - 3)$
$m^2 + 3m = m^2 - 6m + 9 + 3m - 9$
$m^2 + 3m = m^2 - 3m$
$3m = -3m$
$6m = 0$
$m = 0$

5. **D** Just follow the directions.
$(m + 1)(2 - 1) = (5 + 1)(4 - 1)$
$m + 1 = (6)(3)$
$m + 1 = 18$
$m = 17$

Skill 46 (page 103)

Directly Proportional

1. **B** For "y to be directly proportional to x," each y must equal a constant (a number) multiplied by each x. Choice B is correct since each x multiplied by 5 yields each y.

2. **5** "y is directly proportional to x^2" means $\frac{y}{x^2}$. So we set up a proportion between the two sets of (x, y) values, cross-multiply, and solve for the unknown x. Remember Skill 20: when you see a proportion, cross-multiply.

$\frac{y}{x^2} = \frac{y}{x^2} \Rightarrow \frac{18}{3^2} = \frac{50}{x^2}$ cross-multiply

$18x^2 = (9)(50)$
$18x^2 = 450$ divide both sides by 18
$x^2 = 25$ take square root of both
$x = 5$ sides

3. **D** Each y in the table is found by multiplying each x value by 5. So simply multiply $7.5 \times 5 = 37.5$.

4. **B** "y varies directly with x^{-1}" means exactly the same as "y is directly proportional to x^{-1}," so set up a proportion between a pair of numbers in the table and $(5, y)$. Then cross-multiply and solve for y.

$\frac{y}{x^{-1}} = \frac{y}{x^{-1}} \Rightarrow \frac{0.25}{8^{-1}} = \frac{y}{5^{-1}}$ cross-multiply

$8^{-1}y = (5^{-1})(0.25)$
$0.125y = 0.05$ divide both sides
$y = 0.4$ by 0.125

Skill 47 (page 105)

Inversely Proportional

1. **C** "y is inversely proportional to x" implies that $y = \frac{k}{x}$, and therefore $yx = k$. In other words, x times y should equal the same constant for each (x, y) pair in the table. Choice C is correct since x times y for each pair of values equals 108.

2. **E** Just choose an (x, y) pair from the table and try it in each answer choice. The one that works is the right answer. If two work, just try another (x, y) pair as a tie breaker.

3. **A** "y is inversely proportional to x^2" means $y = \frac{k}{x^2}$. Plug the first pair of values into this equation to find the value of k. $16 = \frac{k}{2^2}$. So $k = 64$. Now, using $k = 64$, plug the second pair of values $(x, \frac{1}{2})$ into the equation. $\frac{1}{2} = \frac{64}{x^2}$. Cross-multiply $x^2 = 128$, so $x = \sqrt{128} = \sqrt{64 \times 2} = 8\sqrt{2}$ or 11.3.

4. **C** "y is inversely proportional to x" means $y = \frac{k}{x}$. Plug the first pair of values into this equation to find the value of k. $10 = \frac{k}{3}$. So k = 30. Now, using k = 30, plug the second pair of values (x, 8) into the equation. $8 = \frac{30}{x}$. Cross-multiply 8x = 30, so x = 3.75.

Skill 48 (page 108)

How to Think Like a Math Genius I

1. Proportions (Skill 20). D. When you see a proportion, cross-multiply. 3a = 60, so a = 20.

2. Average (Skill 3). E. The question asks for the sum, so use the sum formula: sum = (average) × (# of items). So sum = (14)(2) = 28.

3. Isosceles triangle (Skill 6) and triangle has 180° (Skill 4). C. If two sides of a triangle are equal, than two angles must also be equal, and since it is a triangle, the measures must add up to 180.

4. Average (Skill 3). 150. Since the average weight of the 5 boys is 120, their sum is (120)(5) = 600. When the sixth boy joins them, their weight cannot exceed 750 pounds, so the sixth boy can weigh up to 750 − 600 = 150.

5. Functions (Skill 15). C. f(b) = 24 means plug in b for x and 24 as the solution:

   $24 = 3(b)^3$ divide by 3
   $8 = b^3$ take cube root of both sides
   $2 = b$

6. Ratios (Skill 19) and proportion (Skill 20). 27. With the ratio of 2 : 3 : 4, there are 9 total pieces of fruit. So set up a proportion for pear to total: $\frac{3}{9} = \frac{9}{x}$ and cross-multiply to solve for x. 81 = 3x, so x = 27.

7. Functions (Skill 14) D. Plug 9 in for M(u) and 6 (since June is the 6th month) in for u, and solve for k.

$9 = ((2)(6))^2 - k$
$9 = 144 - k$
$-135 = -k$
$135 = k$

8. Make It Real (Skill 16) C. "Make It Real" turns this "hard" into an "easy." Choose numbers for the variables. Let's say a = 9 and b = 8. Then
   I works since ab = (9)(8) = 72 which is a multiple of 12.
   II flunks since 3a + 4b = (3)(9) + 4(8) = 59 which is not a multiple of 12.
   III works since 4a + 3b = (4)(9) + (3)(8) = 60 which is a multiple of 12.
   Since this is a late "medium," it's a good idea to test a second set of numbers to confirm that choices I and III both still work.

9. Geometry (Skill 4) and "What is a in terms of b and c?" (Skill 2) D. The best way to solve this question is to realize that the angles marked with a, b's. and c's add up to 360, since they are the four angles of a four-sided shape. Then it's easy since a + 4b + 2c = 360, and we just solve for a.

10. Averages (Skill 3). B. Set up the sum formula for each team. The sum of the first team is 170m, and the sum for the second team is 182m. Now, set up the average formula to determine the average of the groups combined: add the two sums (170m + 182n) and divide by total bowlers (m + n) and set equal to the combined average 177.5. $\frac{170 + 182n}{m + n} = 177.5$.

Algebraically manipulate to get m/n. OK, I admit it, this question is tough. Without our strategies very few students can get it. But our strategies knock it down from nearly impossible to possible.

Skill 49 (page 112)

How to Think Like a Math Genius II

1. Misbehaving Numbers (Skill 43), and Make It Real (Skill 16). A. Negative numbers with larger

digits are smaller. Let's say $m = -3$. Then choice B equals $3m = 3(-3) = -9$. And -3 is actually larger than -9.

2. Misbehaving Numbers (Skill 43), and Make It Real (Skill 16). C. Let's say $p = -3$. $1 - p$ is largest since $1 - p = 1 - (-3) = 4$, while all other answers are negative.

3. Avoid Careless Errors (Skill 41) and Functions (Skill 14). A. Plug n in for x: $m(n) = 2(3n)^2 = 2(9n^2) = 18n^2$. Remember to square the 3 as well as the n, and then multiply by 2.

4. Logic (Skill 36). C. There are 42 yogis and 25 dungeon crawlers, so it would seem there are 67 total; but 18 are in both clubs, and have been counted twice. So at the joint meeting there are really $42 + 25 - 18 = 49$.

5. Translation (Skill 26), and Finish the Question (Skill 42). E. Translate the words into math and solve:

$0.5x - 4 = 0.3x$	add 4 to both sides
$0.5x = 0.3x + 4$	subtract $0.3x$
$0.2x = 4$	divide by 0.2
$x = 20$	remember to finish the question
$3x = 60$	

6. Median and Mode (Skill 34), and Use the Answers (Skill 1). E. When you see a median or mode question, rewrite the data as a list in order. Then try each answer choice. Choice E cannot be the value for p because it will make 7 tied with 3 as the mode.

7. ⓑ Logic (Skill 36) or Make It Real (Skill 16). B. There seem to be $m + p$ total members of sets M and P combined. Usually, we then subtract the common members (r) to determine the total, but in the "hard" question we subtract $2r$ since set Z contains **no** members that are in both. We are not just avoiding double-counting, but eliminating the common members entirely. So, set Z has $m + p - 2r$ members.

8. Arrangements (Skills 31 & 32). 10. Since we have one-on-one competition, we have two

spots to fill, so draw two blanks. Five competitors can fill the first slot, and four can fill the second slot. Then multiply $5 \times 4 = 20$. Because Juan playing Ezra is the same as Ezra playing Juan, we divide by 2 and get $20/2 = 10$.

9. Probability (Skill 33), Donut Area (Skill 18), or Use the Diagram (Skill 21). C. Probability $= \frac{\text{want}}{\text{total}}$, so the probability of hitting the shaded region is $\frac{\text{Want}}{\text{Total}} = \frac{\text{shaded area}}{\text{total area}} = \frac{5^2\pi - 3.5^2\pi}{5^2\pi} = 0.51$.

You could also just "Use the Diagram" and realize that no other answers make sense and that the shaded region being half the area of the larger circle is the only feasible answer.

10. Absolute Value (Skill 38) and Misbehaving Numbers (Skill 43). E. When you see an absolute value question, remember to consider not only the obvious answer, but also the less obvious one. x can equal 7 or -1, and y can equal 1 or -5. So the greatest possible value for $x - y = 7 - (-5) = 12$.

Posttest I (page 119)

1. ⓑ This question looks impossible to some, but "Use the Answers" makes it easy! Try each choice. If $x = 1$, then $8^{1+1} = 2^{1+7}$ or $64 = 256$ which is not true. If $x = 2$, then $8^{2+1} = 2^{2+2}$ or $512 = 512$, so $x = 2$ is correct. Just to be sure, if there is time, you can try each of the other choices to prove that no other choice works and that choice B is correct.

2. ⓑ "What is m in terms of p?" means solve for m, get m alone. Since $2m = 5n = 6p$, we can say that $2m = 6p$. Divide both sides by 2 and $m = 3p$.

3. ⓒ The sum of his grades is $10 \times 82 = 820$. The correct sum should have been 14 points higher (for the 5 and 9 points he was cheated on the 2 test grades). So the correct average is $834/10 = 83.4$, rounded to 83.

4. 142 The angles of any 4-sided closed shape add up to 360, so the 4th angle equals

$360 - 129 - 48 - 145 = 38$, and x forms a linear pair with 38, so $x = 180 - 38 = 142$.

5. **D** In two parallel lines, all big angles are equal and all small angles are equal. Since $x = 53$, it is a small angle. Redraw the diagram to reflect this. Then y is clearly a large angle and must equal $180 - 53 = 127$.

6. **B** As soon as you know that two sides in a triangle are equal, you know that the two angles opposite the two sides are also equal. Therefore, $a = c$. If $b = 160$, then $a + c + 160 = 180$, and $a + c = 20$. Since a equals c, a is half of 20, which is 10.

7. **30** Since $2x$ is the exterior angle of the triangle shown, $2x = x + 30$. Subtract x from both sides to get $x = 30$.

8. **12** Know your vocab terms and try numbers; the numbers can't be too big if they add up to 42. Or, you can divide 42 by 3 to get the middle number, and work from there. $12 + 14 + 16 = 42$.

9. **18** Know your vocab terms and try numbers. The number 36 is the lowest number that is a multiple of 4, 12, and **18**.

10. **C** Don't be intimidated by "xy coordinate plane." It's just the usual grid we use. Same for "ordered pairs," they are just normal (x, y) points. Draw a sketch. Two lines might be parallel and not intersect, or they might intersect in one point, but they cannot intersect twice. To do that, they would have to bend, which unless you live in *The Matrix*, straight lines do not do.

11. **C** Plug the two points into the slope equation:
$$\frac{3-0}{2-(-1)} = \frac{3}{3} = 1$$

12. **C** Parallel lines have equal slopes, so the slope of the line is 3, and slope $= \frac{3-p}{-1-(-2)} = 3$. "Use the Answers" or cross-multiply to solve for p. $p = 0$.

13. **E** The legend tells us that each ♥ represents 20 votes. Therefore, Scary received 90 votes and Posh Spice received 60, and $90 - 60 = 30$. Notice that half a heart equals half of 20, not half of 1.

14. **B** $f(-1) = -3(-1)^2 - 2 = -3 - 2 = -5$

15. **B** This is a very common question on the SAT, showing up very often on recent tests. To solve, simply choose a pair of values such as (2, 6) and plug them into the answer choices for x and $f(x)$ to see in which choice the values work. Remember that $f(x)$ simply means y, so the table of values is a typical (x, y) table. To be sure of your answer, test the pair in all choices. If two answer choices work, choose a second (x, y) pair to determine which one is correct.

16. **C** This question seems theoretical and intimidating to some, but not to us with "Make It Real." Choose a real number in for t (remember, the question says that it must be negative). Let's say $t = -3$. Then try -3 for t in each answer choice to see which one does what the question asks, which one yields a positive number. If you get two or more answers that work, choose another real number for t until you get only one answer choice that works. Choice C is the answer since $3 - (-3) = 6$; in fact, subtracting a negative will always make it positive and that's why this is always the correct answer.

17. **D** Since the radius of circle B is half the diameter of circle A, it must be 8. Therefore, the area of circle B is Area $= \pi r^2 = \pi 8^2 = 64\pi$. You can also just check the scale on the figure, and, if needed, redraw the picture to scale to estimate which answer is correct.

18. **C** Perimeter is the addition of the sides. Since the perimeter of square $BCDF$ is 24, each side is 6. $AB = 12$ and $DE = 4$. Perimeter of the shaded region $= 18 + 4 + 6 + 6 + 12 + 10 = 56$.

19. **D** Remember that 1.4 to 2 is the same as saying "1.4 divided by 2," so just divide 1.4/2 on your calculator to get 0.7. Then divide each answer choice to see which one also gives 0.7. Easy!

20. ⓒ Set up the proportion and cross-multiply.

$\frac{3}{35} = \frac{3.5}{x}$, so $3x = 122.5$. Divide by 3 to get $x =$

40.83 or $40\frac{5}{6}$. If the fractions in the answer

choices scare you, just convert them to decimals.

21. ⓒ Draw point M into the diagram and estimate MD. Using geometry, this is a "hard" question because there are two steps using the Pythagorean theorem. But with "Use the Diagram," it's easy! If AB is 20, BC is 8, and DC is 4, then MD looks like somewhere between 10 and 15, probably in the middle. Translate the answer choices to decimals, and Choice C is correct.

22. ⓑ Easy, if you draw a diagram! The diagram shows that the sides of $ABCD$ are 6, 6, 3, and 7ish. So only answer choice B works.
You could also use the Pythagorean theorem to get the exact length of side CB.

23. ⓑ Use the Pythagorean theorem.
$30^2 + p^2 = 34^2$
$900 + p^2 = 1156$
$p^2 = 256$
$p = 16$

24. ⓑ Draw a diagram. When you see a right triangle, try $a^2 + b^2 = c^2$. You can also use special right triangles if you notice that 3 is half of 6.

25. ⓓ Triangles NBA and NMO are isosceles so base angles are equal. The triangles are similar since they also share a vertex angle ($\angle N$).

26. 115 Translate the words to math and solve.
$3n + 5 = 350$. Subtract 5 from both sides and then divide by 3 to get 115.

27. ⓒ If you see something that can be multiplied, do it. $p(p - 3) = p^2 - 3p$, so $x = p^2 - 3p$. To find $x + 2$, we just add 2 to both sides to get $x + 2 = p^2 - 3p + 2$.

28. ⓔ Good vocab review, "product" means multiply. So $(3bm^4)(2b^4) = 6m^4b^5$. Notice that I did not add the exponents $4 + 4$ because m and b are different letters, and we add only when the letters are the same. Also, notice that the order of the variables does not matter; mb is the same as bm.

29. ⓔ If $b = 2$, then $a^{-3} = (2)^{-9}$ or $a^{-3} = \frac{1}{2^9} =$ 0.002. This is a "hard" question because most students get intimated by the negative exponents, and give up, but with our strategies, it's easy. Just "Use the Answers." Try each answer choice to find which one works. Choice E works since $(8)^{-3} = 0.002$.

30. ⓒ The graph shown represents $y = ax + b$, and we want an answer that shows $y = 3ax + b$. So we want a line that is 3 times steeper than the one in the question, and since b did not change, we want the same y intercept. So choice C is correct.

31. 12 Draw a blank for each option. Then write in the number of possibilities that can fill each option. There are 2 possibilities for slogan, 2 for shirt color, and 3 for size, so
$\underline{2} \times \underline{2} \times \underline{3} = 12$

32. 10 Draw a blank for each member of the pair. Write in the number of people who can fill each blank; remember that once someone is assigned a position, that person cannot also fill the other spot. Then multiply. This question has one extra step. Since this is a team of two and it does not matter if it's Kate and Jack or Jack and Kate, we divide our answer by 2, since we will have double-counted each duo.
$\underline{5} \times \underline{4} = 20 \div 2 = 10$

33. $\frac{1}{2} = 0.5$. Probability $= \frac{\text{want}}{\text{total}}$, so the probability

of selecting a prime number is $\frac{3}{6}$ which reduces

to $\frac{1}{2}$ or 0.5. Remember, you need to reduce to

get credit; the machine would not accept $\frac{3}{6}$ as

the correct answer. Repeat after me, "Reducing is my friend . . ." or just use your calculator to get a decimal.

34. **B** Simply plug each answer in for the variable. If $m = 2$, then the three numbers in the list are 2, 5, 2. $m + 3$, which equals 5, is not the median. But when $m = 4$, the three numbers are 6, 7, 8. Thus, $m + 3$, which equals 7, is the middle number.

35. **A** We love these! Since m is positive, the U-shaped graph must open up and since n is zero, the y intercept must be zero. Choice A is the answer!

36. **C** If all children in the Lederman family are terrific, than obviously there are "no children who are not terrific in the Lederman family." Easy. The only way to get this one wrong is to rush into one of the wrong choices or to doubt yourself and say, "I don't get this, I'll just go with B." But if you stay relaxed and focused and confident, you can easily see why choice C is the correct answer.

37. **D** Nice vocab review. Remember that "consecutive" means in a row, "odd" means numbers like 1, 3, 5, 7, 9, and "integer" means no decimals. So just choose 4 consecutive odd integers and divide each by 3 to see the remainder for each. Depending on the numbers you chose, the correct answer might be in a different order than your numbers.

38. **C** "Use the Answers." Try each answer choice in the equation.

I.	$\lvert 8 - 2 \rvert = 6$	correct
II.	$\lvert -4 - 2 \rvert = \lvert -6 \rvert = 6$	correct
III.	$\lvert -3 - 2 \rvert = \lvert -5 \rvert = 5 \neq 6$	incorrect

So I and II are correct and choice C is the answer.

39. **B** This is sequence question. Continue the sequence until you have seven terms: 6, 10, 18, 34, 66, 130, **258**.

40. **A** Since we add 4 to each new term, by the 57th term, we have added 56 times 4, which equals 224. Thus the 57th term equals 224 plus the original 6, which makes 330.

41. **A** Plug $x = -2$ and simplify. $x(2s^2 - 2) = -2(2s^2 - 2) = -4x^2 + 4$. Careless error buster: Remember to distribute the negative sign!

42. **E** Plug 2 in for x and then FOIL $(y - 2)^2$. You can use the algebra trick for FOILing a binomial if you know it; and if you don't, no sweat, just do it out: $(y - 2)^2 = (y - 2)(y - 2) = y^2 - 2y - 2y + 4 = y^2 - 4y + 4$. Careless error buster: When you FOIL, remember the middle term!

43. **D** Point M is between -4 and -8 on the number line, so D is the only choice that works.

44. **D** This is a straightforward transformation. The parent function $g(x)$ needs to be shifted 1 unit down. If you memorize the transformations, this question is easy; a down transformation would be $y = g(x) - 1$. If you did not memorize the transformations, get to it, you silly slacker. Or, you could graph each choice on your calculator and see which one yields results that are all 1 unit down from the parent.

45. **38** This is a "weird symbol" question. You are not alone; no one has ever seen the symbol for this operation. It's not just because you dropped Precalc to get into Modern Interpretations of Shakespeare class. Just follow the directions given, and it's easy.

$= (3)(6) + (4)(5) = 38$

46. $\frac{20}{3} = 6.66$. "y is directly proportional to x" means $\frac{y}{x}$. So we set up a proportion between the two sets of (x, y) values and solve for the unknown x.

$$\frac{y}{x} = \frac{y}{x} \Rightarrow \frac{21}{4} = \frac{35}{x}$$

$$21x = (4)(35) \Rightarrow 21x = 140 \Rightarrow x = \frac{20}{3} = 6.66$$

On the SAT, you can grid 20/3 or 6.66 or 6.67. You can round or just chop, but when you have a long decimal, you must fill up all four of the grid spaces, i.e., 6.66.

47. Ⓐ "y is inversely proportional to x^2" means

$y = \dfrac{k}{x^2}$. Plug the first pair of values into this

equation to find the value of k. $\dfrac{1}{2} = \dfrac{k}{2^2}$. So,

$2k = 4$ and $k = 2$. Now, using $k = 2$, plug the

second pair of values $(x, \dfrac{1}{8})$ into the equation.

$\dfrac{1}{8} = \dfrac{2}{x^2}$. Cross-multiply $x^2 = 16$, so $x = 4$.

48. Ⓓ There are 2 oranges to every 3 purple crayons, so there are 5 total, or actually some multiple of 5, so choice D is correct.

49. $\dfrac{1}{3} = 0.333$. Probability $= \dfrac{\text{want}}{\text{total}}$, so the probability

of selecting an odd prime number is $\dfrac{2}{6}$ which

reduces to $\dfrac{1}{3}$ or 0.333. Remember, you need

to reduce to get credit, the machine would not

accept $\dfrac{2}{6}$ as the correct answer. Also, you can

grid 1/3 or 0.333, you can round or just chop; but when you have a long decimal, you must fill up all four of the grid spaces, i.e., 0.333.

50. Ⓔ

Glossary

30°, 60°, 90° triangle a triangle with angles that measure 30°, 60°, 90° has sides that measure x, $2x$, and $x\sqrt{3}$. This is shown in the info box at the beginning of every SAT Math section.

45°, 45°, 90° triangle an isosceles right triangle. Its sides have lengths x, x, $x\sqrt{2}$. This is shown in the info box at the beginning of every SAT Math section.

absolute value $|-3|$ means "the absolute value of -3." "Absolute value" means after you do the math between the bars, ditch the negative sign!
- $|-3| = 3$
- $|3| = 3$
- $|-3 - 6| = |-9| = 9$

arithmetic mean anytime the SAT prints the word "average," they follow it with "(arithmetic mean)." This is simply a clarification and a synonym for "average." They are just referring to the normal average that you are used to, so ignore "(arithmetic mean)."

average The "average" of a list of numbers is found by adding them and dividing by how many there are.

$$\text{Average} = \frac{\text{sum}}{\text{number of items}}$$

The SAT also uses the sum formula:

Sum = (avg.) × (# items)

bar graphs graphs that compare the values of several items, such as sales of different toothpastes.

bisect to cut into two equal parts. An angle bisector cuts an angle into two equal parts, and a segment bisector cuts a segment into two equal parts.

careless errors these are bad, "mmmkay."

cartesian plane a fancy term for the normal grid that you graph lines on.

consecutive even/odd numbers even or odd numbers in a row such as 4, 6, 8, 10 or 3, 5, 7, 9.

consecutive numbers numbers in a row such as 7, 8, 9, 10.

constant term this term really throws some kids, but it just means a letter in place of number, kinda like a variable, except that it won't vary.

cross-multiply a method of solving proportions on the SAT. To solve for x in $\frac{5}{12} = \frac{x}{40}$, cross-multiply to get $(5)(40) = 12x$ and divide by 12 to get x alone.

different numbers numbers that are . . . ummm . . . different.

directly proportional also called "direct variation," means "x times some number gives y." The formula for this relationship is $y = kx$.

donut the area of a donut equals the area of the larger circle minus the area of the donut hole.

drawn to scale every diagram on the SAT is drawn to scale unless it states, "Note: Figure not drawn to scale." When a diagram is not drawn to scale, redraw it.

equiangular triangle a triangle with all angles equal, which means that they each must equal 60°. The triangle is therefore also equilateral.

equilateral triangle a triangle with all sides equal and all 60° angles.

even/odd even numbers are 2, 4, 6, 8, . . . ; odd numbers are 1, 3, 5, 7, . . .

exponents, laws of
- $n^6 \times n^2 = n^8$
- $\frac{n^6}{n^2} = n^4$
- $(n^6)^2 = n^{12}$
- $n^0 = 1$
- $n^1 = n$
- $n^{-2} = \frac{1}{n^2}$
- $2n^2 + n^2 = 3n^2$
- $2n + n^2$ does not combine
- $n^{\frac{4}{3}} = \sqrt[3]{n^4}$

exterior angle an angle outside a triangle that equals the sum of the two nonadjacent interior angles.

$x = a + b$

factors numbers that divide into a number evenly (i.e., without a remainder).

Example: The factors of 48 are 1, 2, 3, 4, 6, 8, 12, 16, 24, 48.

1 2 3 4 6 8 12 16 24 48

functions   the cause of much fear in teenagers. A type of equation, like $y = mx + b$. To show that an equation is a function, sometimes people replace the y with $f(x)$ or $g(x)$ or $h(x)$. $f(x)$ is just a fancy way of saying y. So $f(x) = 2x - 1$ means the same as $y = 2x - 1$. $f(3)$ means "plug 3 in for x" and $f(m) = 9$ means, "What did we plug into the equation for x to get a result of 9 ?"

info box   the box of math info and formulas provided at the beginning of every SAT Math section.

integer   a number without decimals or fractions, such as -3, -2, -1, 0, 1, 2, 3, . . . This is the single most common SAT Math vocab word!

inversely proportional   also called "inverse variation," means some number divided by x equals y. The formula is $y = \dfrac{k}{x}$.

isosceles triangle   a triangle with at least two congruent sides. The two angles opposite the two congruent sides are also congruent.

linear pair   two adjacent angles that form a line and add up to 180°.

$m + n = 180$

line graph   display of how data changes, often over time.

"Make It Real."   the strategy to use when you see variables in the question and variables in the answer choices, especially for word problems. Choose real numbers in place of the variables, and the question becomes much easier.

math genius   somebody who has mastered all 50 Skills from *McGraw–Hill's Top 50 Skills for a Top Score: SAT Math.*

median   the middle term in a list of numbers. For the list 2, 5, 7, 8, 8, the number 7 is the median.

mode   the most frequent term in a list of numbers. For the list 2, 5, 7, 8, 8, the number 8 is the mode.

multiples   all the numbers that are divisible by a certain number. The multiples of 3 are 3, 6, 9, 12, 15, 18, 21, etc.

multiple-choice questions   questions that offer answer choices:

Ⓐ
Ⓑ
Ⓒ
Ⓓ
Ⓔ

order of difficulty   questions in SAT Math sections are arranged from easiest to hardest.

ordered pair   a fancy term for a pair of coordinates (x, y) on the xy coordinate plane.

parallel lines   lines in a plane that never intersect and have equal slopes, like $\dfrac{2}{3}$ and $\dfrac{2}{3}$.

perpendicular lines   lines that intersect at a right (90°) angle and have negative reciprocal slopes, like $\dfrac{2}{3}$ and $-\dfrac{3}{2}$.

pictographs   graphs that use small pictures to represent data. The key to pictographs lies in noticing the legend. If each icon represents 8 books, then 1/2 of an icon represents 4 books, not 1/2 of a book.

pie graph   a technique to represent information as part of a pie.

positive/negative numbers positive numbers are greater than 0 and negative numbers are less than 0.

prime factors   the factors of a number that are also prime numbers. The prime factors of 48 are 2 and 3. These are the factors of 48 that also happen to be prime numbers.

prime number   a number whose only factors are 1 and itself, such as 2, 3, 5, 7, 11, 13, 17, 19, . . . The number 1 is NOT considered prime, and the number 2 is the only even prime number.

probability   a measure of the likelihood of something happening. To determine probability on the SAT, use the equation

Probability = $\frac{want}{total}$.

proportion   two ratios set equal to each other, for example, $\frac{5}{12} = \frac{10}{24}$ or $\frac{5}{12} = \frac{x}{40}$. To solve a proportion, cross-multiply.

Pythagorean theorem   when given two sides of a right triangle, we can find the third with the formula $a^2 + b^2 = c^2$.

quadratic equation   an equation with a variable such as x that is squared. For example, $y = ax^2 + bx + c$. In such an equation, the a tells whether the U-shaped graph opens up or down, and c is the y intercept.

ratio   a relationship between two numbers, such as 7 cups of oats to 2 cups of sugar. It can be written as 7 : 2 or $\frac{7}{2}$ or even 7 to 2. The SAT likes to see if you can play with ratios. For example, 4 boys to 5 girls could also be expressed 5 girls to 9 students.

real number   any number, such as -3, -2.2, 0, $\sqrt{2}$, π.

reflection   a mirror image. In the diagram below, line m is the reflection of line l over the x axis. Reflected lines over the x axis or y

axis have negative slopes, like $\frac{2}{3}$ and $-\frac{2}{3}$.

remainders   what's left over when you use long division.

```
     52 r1
7|365
   −35
     15
   −14
      1
```

right triangle   a triangle with a right (90°) angle. When you see a right triangle, use $a^2 + b^2 = c^2$ to find the length of a missing side.

scatterplots   graphs that compare two aspects of a group. When the SAT gives a scatterplot, it often asks you to name the equation of the line that best fits the data. Just sketch a line, estimate its y intercept and slope, and choose the equation (see Skill 30) that matches best.

similar triangles   triangles that have congruent corresponding angles and proportional sides; one is a shrinky version of the other.

slope   the measure of a line's steepness; the steeper the line, the bigger the slope. In the equations

$y = mx + b$ or $y = ax + b$, m or a is the slope, and b is the y intercept.

Slope = $\frac{y_1 - y_2}{x_1 - x_2}$

special right triangles.   a 30°, 60°, 90° triangle with sides x, $2x$, and $x\sqrt{3}$, or a 45°, 45°, 90° triangle with sides x, x, and $x\sqrt{2}$. These are shown in the info box at the beginning of every SAT Math section.

springboard strategy   on the SAT, when something can be factored, FOILed, reduced, or simplified, . . . do it.

student-produced response questions   SAT Math questions that are not followed by answer choices.

tables   charts that display information in rows and columns. Usually the SAT asks you to use the last row or column, which shows totals.

transformation   a change that happens when we add, subtract, multiply, or divide a number into an equation that causes the graph to move up, down, left, or right. It might even make it skinnier or fatter.

translation   conversion of word problems from English to math.

transversal   a line that crosses two parallel lines, forming 8 angles.

triangle a closed shape formed by three sides. The angles in a triangle add up to 180°.

units digit a fancy term for the "ones" digit in a number, like the 2 in 672.

"Use the Answers" a terrific strategy to use when you see <u>variables</u> in the question and <u>numbers</u> in the answers. Try the answer choices for the variables in the question to see which one works.

"Use the Diagram" a great strategy that says since diagrams on the SAT are drawn accurately, we can use the diagrams to estimate the answer to many questions. When the answer choices contain a square root ($\sqrt{\ }$) or the symbol pi (π), always translate to decimals.

vertical angles two angles whose sides form two pairs of opposite rays. Vertical angles are congruent.

$a° = b°$

"what is m in terms of p and q" means solve for m or use algebra to get m alone.

***xy* coordinate plane** a fancy term for the normal *xy* grid that your graph lines on.

Skill 1

When you see **variables** in the question and **numbers** in the answers, . . .

Skill 2

"What is m in terms of p and q" is just a fancy way of saying . . .

Skill 3

When you see the word "average" on the SAT, use . . .

Skill 4

When you see vertical angles, a linear pair, or a triangle, ...

Top 50 Math Skills Flash Cards

Skill 5

When you see two parallel lines that are crossed by another line, eight angles are formed and . . .

When you see **variables** in the question and **numbers** in the answers, "Use the Answers."

"What is m in terms of p and q" is just a fancy way of saying "**solve for m**" or "**use algebra to get m alone**."

When you see the word "average" on the SAT, **usually you need Sum = (average) × (# of items).**

When you see vertical angles, a linear pair, or a triangle, **calculate the measures of all angles.**

When you see two parallel lines that are crossed by another line, eight angles are formed and **all the bigger-looking angles are equal, and all the smaller-looking angles are equal.**

Skill 6

When you see a triangle with two equal sides, . . .

Skill 9

Define the terms "integer," "prime," "factor," "multiple," "units digit," "consecutive."

Skill 7

An exterior angle equals the sum of the . . .

Skill 8

Anytime you see a math vocab term, . . .

Skill 10

What is an ordered pair?

When you see a triangle with two equal sides, **mark the two opposite angles as equal, and when all sides of a triangle are equal, mark all angles 60°.**

An exterior angle equals the sum of the **two far away interior angles**.

Anytime you see a math vocab term, **underline it.**

Integer—numbers without decimals or fractions: −3, −2, −1, 0, 1, 2, 3, . . .

Prime—a number whose only factors are 1 and itself. 2, 3, 5, 7, 11, 13, 17, . . . are prime. *Note:* The number 1 is NOT considered prime, and the number 2 is the only even prime number.

Factors—numbers that divide into a number evenly (i.e., without a remainder). Example: The factors of 48 are 1, 2, 3, 4, 6, 8, 12, 16, 24, 48.

Multiples—all the numbers that are divisible by a certain number. Example: The multiples of 3 are 3, 6, 9, 12, 15, 18, 21, etc.

Units digit—just a fancy term for the "ones" digit in a number, like the 2 in 672.

Consecutive numbers—numbers in a row: 7, 8, 9, 10.

"Ordered pair" is a fancy term for a pair of coordinates (x, y) on the xy coordinate plane.

Skill 11

The slope of a line measures its steepness; the steeper the line, the _____ the slope.

Skill 12

Parallel lines have _____ slopes.
Perpendicular lines have _____ slopes.
Reflections have _____ slopes.

Skill 13

The key to understanding tables and graphs is to read the . . .

Skill 14

$f(3)$ means . . .

Skill 15

$f(m) = 9$ means . . .

The slope of a line measures its steepness; the steeper the line, the **bigger** the slope.

$f(3)$ means **"plug 3 in for x."**

Parallel lines have **equal** slopes.

Perpendicular lines have **negative reciprocal** slopes.

Lines reflected over the x axis or y axis have **negative** slopes

$f(m) = 9$ means **"What did we plug into the equation for x to get a result of 9?"**

The key to understanding tables and graphs is to read the **headings and the legend if there is one**.

Skill 16

When you see **variables** in the question and **variables** in the answer choices, especially for word problems, use . . .

Skill 17

What information is provided in the info box at the beginning of every SAT Math section?

Skill 18

The area of a donut equals . . .

Skill 19

4 boys to 5 girls could also be expressed as . . . .

Skill 20

When you see a proportion on the SAT, ...

When you see **variables** in the question and **variables** in the answer choices, especially for word problems, **use "Make It Real."**

Area of triangle, rectangle, circle
Volume of solid
Circumference of circle
Special right triangles
Pythagorean theorem
360° in a circle
180° in a triangle

The area of a donut equals **the area of the big guy minus the area of the donut hole.**

4 boys to 5 girls could be expressed as
4 to 5
4 : 5
4/5
4 boys to 9 total students
or 5 girls to 9 total students

When you see a proportion on the SAT, **cross-multiply.**

Skill 21

"Use the Diagram" to estimate an answer. Translate into decimals any answer choices that contain _____

Skill 24

When you see a 30°, 45°, or 60° angle in a right triangle, try using . . . .

Skill 22

When a diagram is not drawn to scale, ... When a picture is described but not shown, . . .

Skill 23

When you see a right triangle, try . . .

Skill 25

Similar triangles have sides that are . . .

Translate into decimals any answer choices that contain $\sqrt{\ }$ **or** π.

When a diagram is not drawn to scale, **redraw it**. When a picture is described but not shown, **draw it!**

When you see a right triangle, try $a^2 + b^2 = c^2$.

When you see a 30°, 45°, or 60° angle in a right triangle, try using **the special right triangles.**

Similar triangles have sides that are **proportional.**

Skill 26

Translate the following from English to math: Ten less than twice a number is four.

Skill 27

When something can be factored, FOILed, reduced, or simplified, . . .

Skill 28

Name the laws of exponents.

Skill 29

$n^{-3/4} =$

Skill 30

For the equation $y = mx + b$ or $y = ax + b$, m or a is the _____ and b is the _____.

$2x - 10 = 4$

When something can be factored, FOILed, reduced, or simplified, . . . **do it!**

$n^6 \times n^2 = n^8 \qquad \dfrac{n^6}{n^2} = n^4$

$(n^6)^2 = n^{12} \qquad n^0 = 1$

$n^1 = n \qquad n^{-2} = \dfrac{1}{n^2}$

$2n^2 + n^2 = 3n^2 \qquad 2n + n^2 \quad$ does not combine

$n^{4/3} = \sqrt[3]{n^4}$

$n^{-3/4} = \dfrac{1}{\sqrt[4]{n^3}}$

For the equation $y = mx + b$ or $y = ax + b$, m or a is the <u>slope</u> and b is the **y intercept.**

Skill 31

When you see an arrangement question, . . .

Skill 32

When an arrangement question mentions a restriction, . . .

When an arrangement question mentions a pair or team, . . .

Skill 33

When you see "probability," use the equation . . .

Skill 34

When you see "median" or "mode," rewrite the data as . . . .

Skill 35

For the equation $y = ax^2 + bx + c$, the a tells . . . , and the c is the _____.

When you see an arrangement question, **draw a blank for each position, fill in the # of possibilities to fill each position, and multiply**.

When an arrangement question mentions a restriction, **fill in the restricted positions first**.

When an arrangement question mentions a pair or team, **divide your result by 2**.

When you see "probability," use the equation **Probability** $= \frac{\text{want}}{\text{total}}$.

When you see "median" or "mode," **rewrite the data as a list in order**.

For the equation $y = ax^2 + bx + c$, the a tells whether the **U-shaped graph opens up or down**, and the c is the y **intercept**.

Skill 36

There are 10 members of the Spanish Club and 10 members of the Ski Team, but 3 people belong to both. If the Spanish Club and Ski Team hold a joint meeting, how many people will attend?

Skill 39

To solve a sequence question, write the next bunch of terms until you have . . .

Skill 37

Remainders are what's left over when you . . .

Skill 38

When you see absolute value, look for . . .

Skill 40

The 59th term in the repeating sequence 7, 3, 1, 0, 7, 3, 1, 0, 7, . . . is

10 + 10 − 3 = 17 people will attend.

Remainders are what's left over when you **use long division**.

When you see absolute value, look for **both answers**.

Example: $|x − 3| = 5$
The answers are 8 and −2.

To solve a sequence question, write the next bunch of terms until you have **as many as you need or until you see a repeating pattern**.

The 59th term in the repeating sequence 7, 3, 1, 0, 7, 3, 1, 0, 7, … is 1.

Skill 41

$$\frac{25x^3 - 18}{5x} = ?$$

Skill 44

Name seven mathematical transformations.

Skill 42

Careless errors are bad, "mmmkay,"

so _____ all vocabulary words and . . .

Skill 43

Name five weird number behaviors.

Skill 45

When you see a weird symbol question, ...

$$\frac{25x^3 - 18}{5x} = \frac{25x^3 - 18}{5x}$$

This expression does not reduce, since the $5x$ is "under" both the $25x^3$ and the 18.

Careless errors are bad, "mmmkay," so **underline** all vocabulary words and **remember to finish the question**.

1. Small fractions multiplied by small fractions get smaller.
2. The larger the digits of a negative number, the smaller it actually is. Example: $-6 < -1$
3. Subtracting a negative number is like adding. Example: $10 - (-4) = 14$
4. Squaring a negative eliminates it, but cubing does not. Example: $(-3)^2 = 9$, but $(-3)^3 = -27$
5. Anything times zero equals zero.

Equation	Effect
$y = x^2 + 1$	moves every point of the graph up 1 unit
$y = x^2 - 1$	moves every point of the graph down 1 unit
$y = (x + 1)^2$	moves every point of the graph left 1 unit
$y = (x - 1)^2$	moves every point of the graph right 1 unit
$y = 2(x)^2$	makes the graph skinnier
$y = 0.5(x)^2$	makes the graph fatter
$y = -(x)^2$	reflects the graph

When you see a weird symbol question: **1) relax, 2) remember that no one has seen this symbol before, and 3) follow the directions given in the question.**

Skill 46

"Directly proportional" means . . .

Skill 47

"Inversely proportional" means . . .

Skill 48

Name at least 10 SAT Math Skills.

Skill 49

Name at least 10 more SAT Math Skills.

Skill 50

Are you prepared?

"Directly proportional" means "*x* **times some number gives *y*.**"

It can be expressed as $y = kx$.

"Inversely proportional" means "**some number divided by *x* equals *y*.**"

It can be expressed as $y = \frac{k}{x}$ or $xy = k$.

Answers vary; use any of these cards.

Answers vary; use any of these cards.

YES!